Clothes for Children

making new from old

Maureen Goldsworthy

Clothes for Children
making new from old

B. T. Batsford Ltd London

Acknowledgment

The author wishes to express her gratitude to Katie Batten, Airlie and Iona Scott, James and David Longman and baby Elizabeth Davis who modelled the clothes with such panache, and to Mr Robert Saunders for his lively photographs taken, by kind permission of Mrs P.A. Nesbitt and Mr A.V. Robinson, at the Doll Museum, Warwick.

Note

Throughout the book, shading in the line illustrations indicates the right side of fabric, as in commercial dress patterns

For M.D.

First published 1980
© Maureen Goldsworthy 1980

ISBN 0 7134 2041 3

Printed in Great Britain by Anchor Press Ltd
Tiptree, Essex
for the publishers B.T. Batsford Ltd,
4 Fitzhardinge Street, London W1H 0AH

Contents

1 Christening robe in moiré, from a wedding dress

Introduction

Something for nothing appeals to all of us, especially to mothers of young children whose clothes eat up an ever-larger proportion of the family budget. After all, the less we need to spend on children's clothes, the more there is left to spend on their shoes, or even on something new for ourselves.

The clothes shown in this book were all made from discarded adult garments or from dressmaking scraps. They are just some examples of the great variety of clothes – sturdy and practical, or pretty for parties, or warm and weatherproof – that you can make easily, quickly and with no great sewing skill. They will not cost you a penny.

You begin quite simply by looking out all those garments that hang perennially unworn at the back of a wardrobe, or clutter up the bottom of a drawer. The most unpromising adult garments – old jeans and trousers, T-shirts, sweaters and skirts – are ideal for making into children's heavy-duty clothes. Plentiful in most households, these rejected garments – still good in most parts, or at any rate on the wrong side of the fabric – provided the raw material for many of the clothes shown in this book.

At the other end of the scale, you may have a cherished but unfashionable dress of beautiful material which could be transformed into a little girl's party dress. Consider even your own wedding dress; it could very appropriately be cut into a splendid family Christening Robe like the one shown opposite.

Other sources of material are jumble sales – the hunting ground of the alertly conservation-minded, where one should look out for large-sized garments with plenty of yardage – and those scraps left over from one's own dressmaking which, even if not big enough for whole garments, can give interesting contrast in yokes or pockets.

Once you begin to look critically at adult clothes as a source of new ones for children, ideas for styles follow easily. Bought patterns can of course be used, but as well as being expensive they tend to be extravagant with fabric. The patterns for the twenty styles in this book, each in several sizes, have been designed to fit economically onto the sometimes limited width of material available, particularly from such garments as trousers. They are not difficult to copy from the diagrams and do not need squared drafting paper.

There is one great difference between ordinary dressmaking and re-making. You will not be starting out with a length of uncut fabric, so you must place the pattern pieces, not in a regular layout, but on those parts of the garment where there happens to be room for them. You may well find yourself short of fabric; there are several ways round this problem. You may find that the pattern pieces are too long or too wide to fit in; then you *add a seam* as part of the style. For example, a bodice can be cut in two parts with a seam at the yoke, or a skirt cut with more but narrower panels. (Instructions for adding seams are given on page 110). On the other hand, you may find that a seam in the original garment lies just where you need to place a pattern piece; then use that seam in your design. For instance, a child's jeans could retain the side seam of adult trousers. (See page 111 for instructions.) Another possibility, for the larger sizes, is to use two old garments to supply plenty of material for one new one; the contrasting colours or textures could add liveliness and interest to the design.

Ingenuity can stretch the available fabric quite surprisingly far, but there is one point to watch. In ordinary dressmaking the pattern pieces are laid parallel to the selvedge, so that the direction of the thread runs down the centre of bodice, sleeve, skirt or trouser section. In laying a pattern on an existing garment, without the help of the selvedge, you must still be careful to follow the same grain direction. If cut off-grain, the finished garment would not hang evenly, or might droop at one side of the hemline. It helps to run a line of tacking or to press a crease down the garment section, to give yourself a true grain-line; the directional arrows of the pattern can then be laid parallel to it *(figure 1)*.

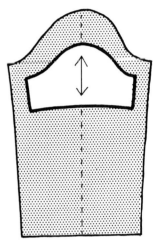

Figure 1

The Patterns

The patterns include all seam and hem allowances. They are cut to the British Standards Institution sizing, which is based on the child's height.

The size for your child

To find the right pattern size, take these measurements:
Height without shoes ....cm
Nape of neck to back of knee ....cm
Waist to ground (taken down the side) ....cm
Chest (closely but not tightly) ....cm
Waist (closely but not tightly) ....cm
Hip (closely but not tightly) ....cm

Check these measurements with the Size Chart below and *choose the size that corresponds to the child's height.* For little girls' dresses, the measurement from nape to knee is the most valuable one; for trousers, the measurement from waist to ground.

If the pattern size that suits your child's height is not wide enough around the chest, tummy or hips, extra width can be added quite easily as shown on page 111.

In the pattern instructions for each style, the measurements for the smallest size are given first; those for the larger sizes are given in brackets following.

The size chart (Measurements in centimetres)

Size No. (Approx. age)	2	3	4	5	6	7	8	9	10	11
Height	92	98	104	110	116	122	128	134	140	146
Nape of neck to knee	51	54	57	61	65	69	72	76	80	84
Waist to ground	56	60	64	68	72	77	81	85	89	93
Chest	53	55	57	59	61	63	66	69	72	76
Waist	52	53	54	55	57	58	59	61	62	63
Hip	56.5	59	61	63.5	66	68	71.5	75	78.5	83

Drafting the patterns

You will need a tape measure marked in centimetres, a long ruler or straight edge, and a supply of plain paper in large sheets. Brown wrapping paper or wall lining paper are ideal.

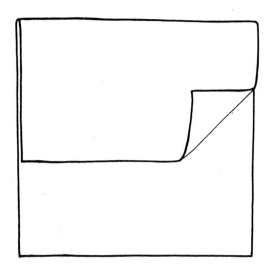

Figure 2

The system used in this book takes a rectangle of paper for each pattern piece; the various measurements are then marked round its edges and the marks joined up to give the pattern outline. This is an accurate and simple method, but it does require that the sides of the paper rectangles should be precisely at right angles to each other. The best way to achieve this is to fold and crease a length of paper across its width, matching the side edges *(figure 2)*. Cut along the crease to give accurate right angles at the corners.

Preparing to cut out

Open up the seams and let down the hem of the garment. Press, to restore the shape of the sections. If the fabric needs to be washed or dry-cleaned, it should be done now, in pieces.

Mark a tailor's chalk line – or press a crease – down the centre of each piece to show the direction of the thread. It is important that the grain-arrows on the pattern pieces are placed parallel to these markings.

Christening Robe
from a Wedding Dress

If your wedding dress will translate into an evening dress, well and good; many will not. Nor can you be sure that your daughter will want to wear it in twenty years' time. A more exciting and equally appropriate idea would be to make it into a family Christening Robe that could become an heirloom.

The robe shown on page 6 and at the left of *figure 3* can be made from the stiffest satin or brocade; yet the variation of the pattern in the right-hand sketch would be suitable for thin, soft or sheer fabrics. The robe was designed to hang generously full, but to fit comfortably round the baby's chest. It is a coat shape, buttoning only at the back of the bodice; so the skirt, falling free, hangs better and is more practical. The neckline and wrist edges are

Figure 3

11

finished with a plain binding of the fabric, as lace or other decoration here can be irritating and may get messy; in any case, babies' necks are invisible.

On the skirt, with plenty of space, you can combine beautiful material with lavish decoration. You could use rows of tucks or faggoting, frills of broderie anglaise or lace, inset bands of lace, machine or hand embroidery, or any permutation of these spaced down the skirt.

In spite of its sumptuous appearance, this pattern is very simple to draft and make up.

Drafting the pattern

The back

Cut a rectangle of paper 95cm long by 42cm wide. Mark A at the top left-hand corner and B and the bottom right-hand corner, as in *figure 4*.
Measuring along the top edge:
A – C is 5.5
A – D is 11
A – E is 18
A – F is 23.5

G is 1 below A
H is 1.5 below C
J is 8.5 below E
K is 11 below F
Measuring up the right-hand edge, L is 5 above B
Measuring along the bottom edge, M is 28 to the left of B
Join G – H – D in a shallow curve for the neckline
Join D – J – K for the raglan armhole (D – J is a straight line; J – K is a shallow curve)
Join K – L for the side seam
Join L – M in a smooth line for the hem
Cut out, discarding the shaded areas
Mark a straight-grain arrow parallel to the left-hand edge

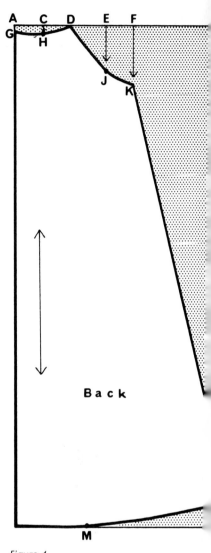

Figure 4

The front

Cut a rectangle of paper 95cm long by 36cm wide
Mark A at the top right-hand corner and B at the bottom left-hand corner, as in *figure 5*.
Measuring along the top edge:
A – C is 2
A – D is 5
A – E is 12
A – F is 17.5

G is 5 below A
H is 4.5 below C
J is 8.5 below E
K is 11 below F
Measuring up the left-hand edge, L is 5 above B

Measuring along the bottom edge, M is 25 to the right of B
Join G – H – D in a full curve for the neckline
Join D – J – K for the armhole. (D – J is a straight line;
J – K is curved)
Join K – L for the side seam
Join L – M in a smooth line for the hem
Cut out, discarding the shaded areas
Mark a fold-arrow down the right-hand edge

The sleeves

Cut a rectangle of paper 25.5cm long by 31cm wide
Mark the corners A, B and C as shown in *figure 6*
Measuring along the top edge:

A – D is 7
A – E is 13
A – F is 16.5
A – G is 19
A – H is 24

J is 7.5 below D
K is 2 below F
L is 1.5 below G
M is 8 below H

Measuring up the left-hand edge, N is 13.5 above B
Measuring along the bottom edge:
B – P is 4.5
B – Q is 16

R is 0.5 above Q
Measuring up the right-hand edge, S is 13.5 above C
T is 4 to the left of C along the bottom edge
Join N – J – E for the back of the armhole. (N – J is curved;
J – E is a straight line)
Join E – K – L for the neckline
Join L – M – S for the front of the armhole. (L – M is a straight
line; M – S is curved)
Join N – P and S – T in shallow curves for the sleeve seam
Join P – R – T for the hemline
Cut out, discarding the shaded areas
Mark a straight-grain arrow down the centre of the pattern

Adapting the pattern for a robe in stiff fabric

You may be able to fit the whole front pattern on a single
panel of the wedding dress, but the robe will gain immeasur-
ably in interest and design possibilities if the front is cut in three
sections, the centre one to be richly decorated.

1 Crease the front pattern from H to M and cut along the crease
figure 7). Add seam allowances along both cut edges, as shown
on page 110.

2 Fold the side-front pattern in half lengthwise, matching

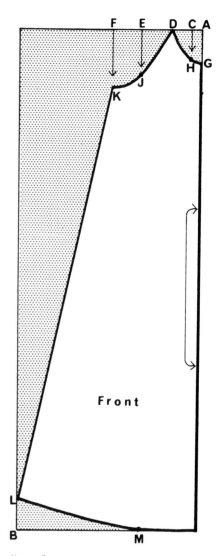

Figure 5

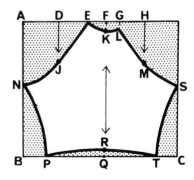

Figure 6

13

together the side edges, and crease. Mark a straight-grain arrow down the crease.

3 If you plan to use tucks for decoration, you will need to lengthen the centre-front pattern. Place it over a folded piece of paper, matching the centre-front of the pattern to the fold *(figure 8)*. Estimate the extra length needed for tucks; each small tuck will take up 1cm of length, or each pin-tuck 3mm. Multiply by the number of tucks, and add that length to the pattern. The dotted line indicates the extra length added, and the width of the seam allowance. Cut out and unfold the new pattern. Mark a straight-grain arrow down the fold.

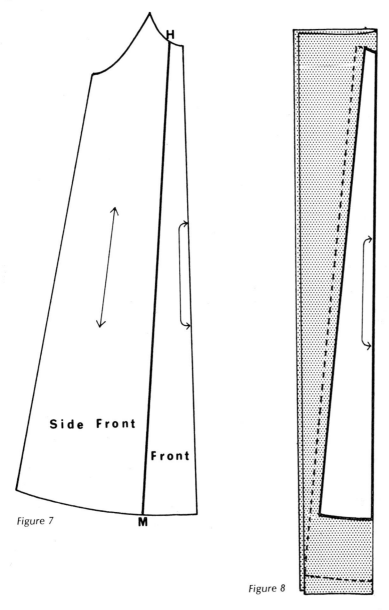

Figure 7

Side Front

Front

Figure 8

Adapting the pattern for a robe in soft fabric

By adding a seam at underarm level, the skirt of the robe can be gathered into a yoke, as in *figure 3*. In crêpe, voile, soft lace or any thin material, this will give a prettier line.

On a patterned fabric, no decoration would be needed on the skirt, which could be finished with lace at the hem. But horizontal bands of lace or frilling would be enchanting on a plain fabric, combined with hand or machine embroidery. Some ideas are shown on page 18.

1 On the back pattern, mark these points, as shown in *figure 9*:
N is 19cm below G, down the centre-back
P is 20 below D
Q is 6 below K, down the side edge
Join N – P – Q in a smooth line
Cut off and discard the lower part of the pattern

2 On the front pattern, mark these points, as shown in *figure 10*:
N is 15cm below G, down the centre-front
P is 20 below D
Q is 6 below K, down the side edge
Join N – P – Q in a smooth line
Cut off and discard the lower part of the pattern

3 The skirt needs no paper pattern. It is cut 78cm long. The fullness should depend on the fabric; it should be not less than 150cm in circumference but, with fabric thin enough to gather really well, the skirt could be as wide as 180 or 200cm if you have enough material available.

The skirt is cut in one piece from the skirt of the wedding dress, across any existing seams. If the dress skirt is gathered and cut entirely on the straight, then the skirt of the robe will be a rectangle; but if the dress skirt was flared, then you should retain the flare to give greater width at the hemline. The skirt piece (including existing seams) will then have the shape shown in *figure 11*.

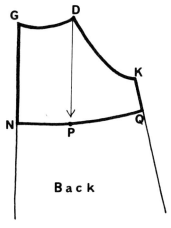

Back

Figure 9

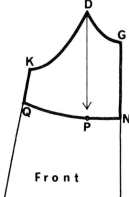

Front

Figure 10

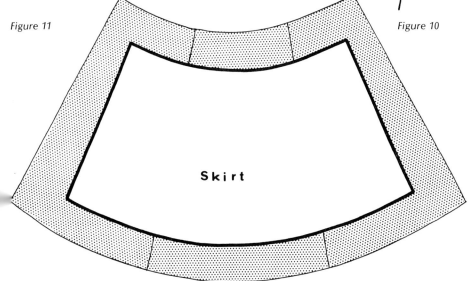

Figure 11

Skirt

15

Cutting out

No pattern layout is given, as you will have plenty of fabric in the wedding dress for either version of the robe.

Pin the pattern pieces to the fabric, right sides up, matching the arrows to the straight thread of the fabric. Be sure to turn over the pieces before cutting the left back, left sleeve etc.

Making up the robe in stiff fabric

You will need: 3 metres of bias binding and 4 small buttons
Seam allowance: 1.5cm

1 First work any tucks, insertions or embroidery on the centre-front panel. On the robe in the photograph, the front panel was entirely covered with bands of lace, hemmed in place along the upper edge and left free along the lower. You should plan out the best spacing for the lace – or other decoration – on the paper pattern, before beginning any sewing.

2 Join the centre-front to the side-front pieces with plain seams *(figure 12)*, which will take in the ends of the lace strips. Finish these seams narrowly with bias binding. (Instructions on page 112.)

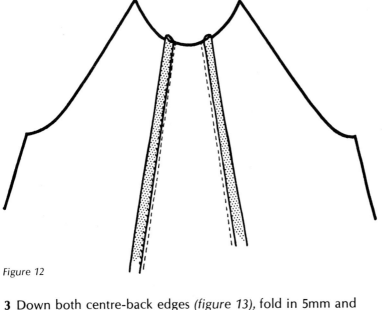

Figure 12

3 Down both centre-back edges *(figure 13)*, fold in 5mm and finish with machine stitching. Fold the stitched edges to the inside to form 5cm facings, and tack down.

4 On the right back, work four machine-buttonholes through both thicknesses, as shown in *figure 13*. Make them 1cm from the folded edge, and at these distances from the neckline: 1cm, 5cm, 9cm, 13cm. Instructions on page 116.

Figure 13

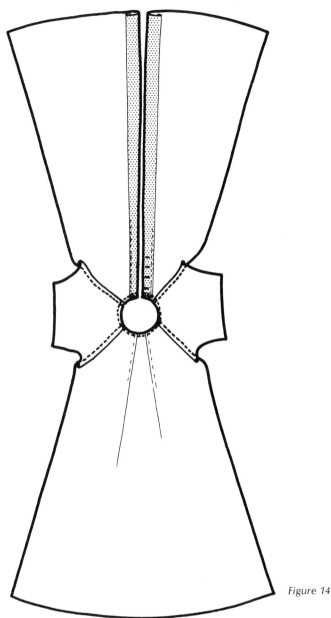

Figure 14

5 Join the sleeve back edges (E – N, *figure 6*) to the backs of the robe with French seams; see page 113.

6 Join the sleeve front edges to the side-fronts with French seams *(figure 14)*.

7 Run a line of machine stitching round the whole neckline, 5mm from the raw edge, taking in the facings of the back opening. (This strengthening will be hidden by binding.)

8 Bind the neckline with bias binding cut from the garment fabric or, if this is too heavy and stiff, with binding cut from any soft, silky material.

9 Stitch the sleeve and side seams as one long French seam *(figure 15)*. This must be kept very narrow under the armhole.

10 Bind the wrist edges of the sleeves to match the neckline.

11 Finish the lower edge of the robe with lace, with a frill or with a narrow hem. See page 114 for instructions.

12 Sew on buttons to the left back, to correspond to the button-holes.

Making up the robe in soft fabric

You will need: 2 metres of bias binding and 4 small buttons
Seam allowance: 1.5cm

The bodice

Follow instructions 3 and 5-10 on pages 16-18, as for the previous robe. Omit the buttonholes for the present.

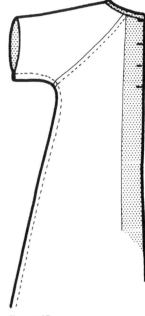

Figure 15

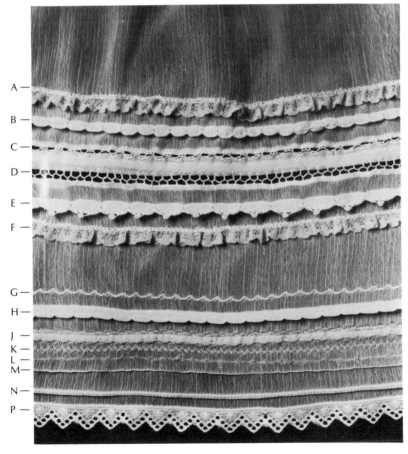

2 Examples of decorative stitching suitable for a christening robe in soft fabric:

By hand
A   Gathered lace applied with chain-stitch
B   Shell-stitched tuck
C   Buttonhole insertion stitch, to insert a ribbon or rouleau
D   Faggoting stitch, to insert a ribbon or rouleau
E   Tuck, shell-edged with buttonhole stitch and bullion picots
F   Gathered lace, applied with chain-stitch

By machine
G   Machine scallop-stitch
H   Tuck, shell-edged with the blind-hemming stitch
J   Ribbon applied with machine embroidery stitching
K   Zig-zag stitch with twin-needle
L   Machine embroidery stitching
M   Pin-tuck
N   Pin-tuck with twin-needle
P   Eyelet embroidery attached with machine satin stitch

The skirt

1 Plan and apply any bands of decoration round the whole skirt. Their number, width and spacing are all-important to the finished style of the robe, so first experiment with different arrangements of threads, ribbon and lace. Photograph 2 shows examples of decorative borders worked by hand and machine. (NB Tucks are difficult to work if the skirt is flared.) When you are satisfied with the design, mark the placing of the bands with tacking, measuring from the top or bottom edge of the skirt, to be sure that they are level all round. Work the decorative bands.

2 Turn in and machine 5mm down each centre-back edge, to finish the edge.

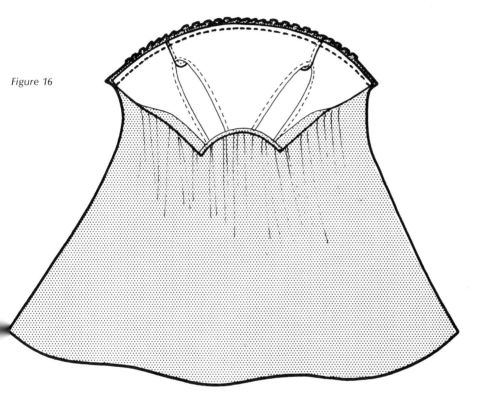

Figure 16

3 Finish the hem with gathered lace or a frill. (Page 114).

4 Follow the instructions on page 113 for gathering the upper edge of the skirt. Pull up the gathering threads to fit the bodice with its facings opened out; tack together and stitch. There should be no gathers in the facings *(figure 16)*. Finish the seam with bias binding.

5 Turn in and press 5cm facings at each side of the centre-back opening, to match the bodice facings. Catch the facings back at the hem.

6 Work the buttonholes, following the instructions for the previous robe. Sew buttons to the left back.

Tabard from Miniskirt

Sizes 2/3 (4/5, 6/7)

This useful little cover-up can be made in any firm washable material. The one shown on the right on page 24 was in tweed (already well-washed to prevent any further shrinkage) and was lined with scarlet heavy cotton – actually from an old table-cloth. As the fit is provided by ribbon ties at the waist, this tabard will grow with its wearer. Pockets on both the outside and the lining make it fully reversible.

Drafting the pattern

Cut a rectangle of paper 47 (53, 61) cm long by 18 (19, 20) cm wide, as in *figure 17*
Mark A at the top left-hand corner
Measure down the left-hand side:
A – B is 5 (6, 7)
A – C is 10 (11, 12)
A – D is 13 (14, 15)

Mark E at the bottom left-hand corner
Measure across the top edge:
A – F is 7.5 (8, 8.5)
A – G is 13.5 (14, 14.5)

H is 1.5cm below G in all sizes
J is 6 (6.5, 7) to the right of B
K is 10.5 (11.5, 12.5) to the right of D
Mark L on the right-hand edge, 30 (31, 32) down from the top corner
Join C – J – F for the neckline. (C – J is well curved, but J – F is almost a straight line.)
Join F – H for the shoulder line
Join H – K – L – E for the outer edge of the tabard. (Hollow out the line between H and K, curve it out to L and draw a fat curve, almost a quarter circle, from L to E.)
Cut out, discarding the shaded areas
Mark a fold-arrow down the left-hand side

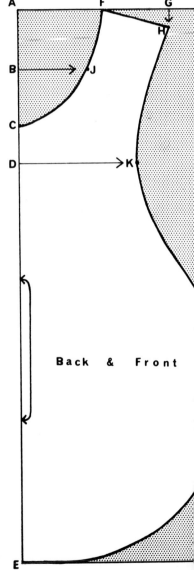

Back & Front

Figure 17

Cutting out

Figure 18 shows the layout suggested if you are cutting out from a skirt. Place the fold-arrow to a fold of the fabric, and cut out through the two thicknesses.

Cut the back to the same pattern. The patch pocket is a 13 (14, 15) cm square, curved off at the two lower corners.

From contrasting fabric, cut the lining and lining pocket to the same pattern.

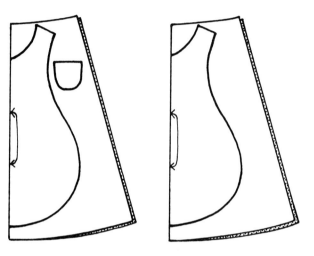

Figure 18

Making up the tabard

1 You will need 1 metre of ribbon for the waist ties.
Seam allowances: 1cm only

2 Stitch the shoulder seams. Make sure that the head opening is large enough to slip on easily. If not, trim it fractionally lower.

3 Fold the top edge of the pocket to the right side in a 2.5cm facing. Stitch the short seams at each side *(figure 19)*.

4 Turn the facing through to the wrong side and press in the pocket turnings *(figure 20)*.

5 Try on the tabard and pin the pocket at the level that looks best. Top-stitch in place.

6 Pin a 25cm ribbon tie at each side of the back and front, at the child's waist level *(figure 21)*.

7 Make up the lining and lining pocket in the same way.

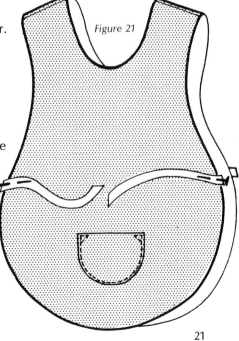

Figure 21

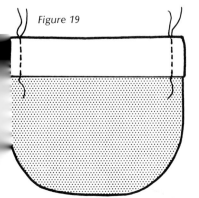

Figure 19

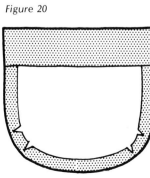

Figure 20

21

8 Place the tabard and lining with right sides together and stitch a continuous seam all round the outer edge. The ties should lie between the two layers of fabric, and their ends should be taken into the seam *(figure 22)*. Clip the seam turnings at curves.

9 Turn right side out through the neck opening and press.

10 Tack the tabard and lining together round the neckline. Finish with bias binding cut from the lining fabric. See page 112 for instructions on bias binding.

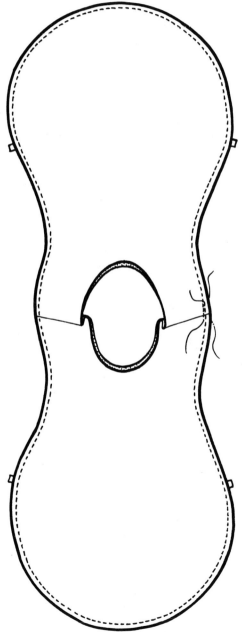

Figure 22

Popover from Corduroy Trousers

Sizes 2 (3, 4)

Either a boy or a girl could wear this top with pants. It is designed to give plenty of ease over thick jerseys, as shown on the left in photograph 3.

Drafting the pattern

Cut a rectangle of paper 45 (48, 51) cm long by 24 (25, 26) cm wide, as in *figure 23*.
Mark A at the top left-hand corner
Measure down the left-hand edge:
A – B is 4 (4.3, 4.5)
A – C is 9.5 in all sizes
A – D is 13.5 (14, 14.5)
A – E is 17.5 (18, 18.5)

Mark F at the bottom left-hand corner
Measure across the top edge:
A – G is 7 (7, 7.5)
G – H is 5cm in all sizes

J is 1.5 below H in all sizes
K is 4 (4.5, 5) to the right of C
L is 6.5 to the right of K in all sizes
M is 18.5 (19, 19.5) to the right of E
Mark N on the right-hand edge, 2cm above the bottom corner
Join B – G in a good curve for the back neckline
Join D – K – G for the front neckline. (D – K is almost a quarter-circle; K – G is a straight line)
Join G – J for the shoulder line
Join J – L – M for the armhole (J – L is slightly hollowed; L – M is almost a quarter-circle)
Join M – N for the side seam
Draw a shallow curve between F and N for the hemline
Cut out the back pattern (higher neckline) and discard the shaded areas. From this pattern, trace on another piece of paper the outline of the front pattern and cut the lower front neckline.
Mark a fold-arrow down the left-hand side of both patterns

3 Tabard from miniskirt *(right)* and popover from corduroy trousers

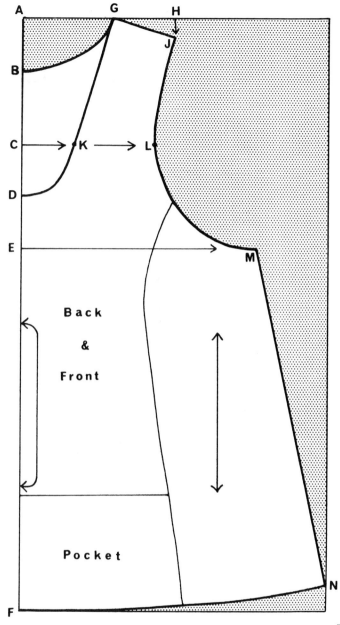

A

G H

B

C → K → L

D

E →

B a c k

&

F r o n t

P o c k e t

M

J

N

F

Figure 23

Cutting out

The popover opposite was made from trousers which were not,
of course, wide enough to take the whole back or front patterns.
So seams were added; instructions for this are on page 110.

The back was given a centre seam; the front was split into three
panels, the centre one being as wide as the trousers would allow.
This side-front seam can be drawn in any position you wish, but

25

will look best if it is curved inwards for the top third of its length. Mark a straight-grain arrow on the side-front pattern.

Trace the pocket shape from the centre-front pattern, making it 15cm deep. Place the centre-front of the pattern to a fold of the fabric when cutting out.

Figure 24 shows the layout suggested on trousers. You can get more hem-width by turning the trouser pieces upside-down; but on corduroy be sure that *all* the pattern pieces are laid in the same direction so that the nap of the fabric does not produce a parti-coloured effect.

Making up the popover

1 You will need 1.5 metres of contrasting bias binding for the armholes, neckline and pocket; and 1 metre of matching bias binding for the hem.
Seam allowances: 1.5cm. Hem allowance: 3cm

2 Tack a strip of contrasting bias binding, folded in half length-wise, down the centre of the pocket. Finish the top and bottom edges of the pocket with zig-zag stitching *(figure 25)*.

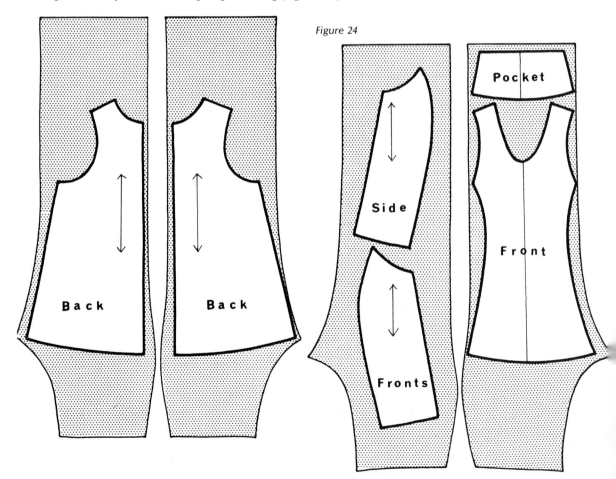

Figure 24

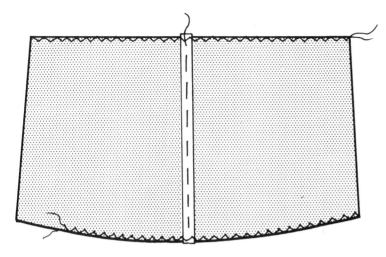

Figure 25

3 Turn under 2.5cm along the top and 1.5cm along the bottom of the pocket, and press.

4 Top-stitch the lower edge of the pocket 3cm above the lower edge of the front panel *(figure 26)*.

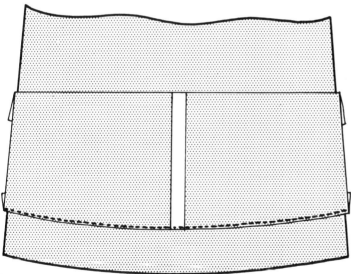

Figure 26

5 Stitch the side-front seams, taking in the sides of the pocket. Stitch down each edge of the binding, to divide the pocket in two *(figure 27)*.

6 Stitch the centre-back seam, shoulder seams and side seams. Finish the seam edges with zig-zag stitching.

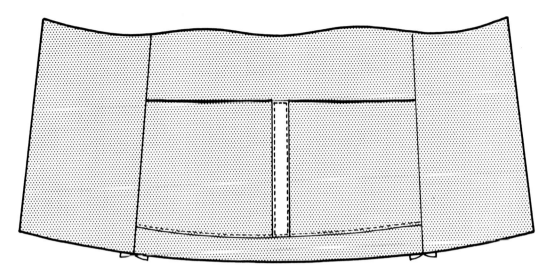

Figure 27

7 Try on the popover, to make sure the neck opening is large enough. If not, trim it slightly lower in front.

8 Bind the neckline and armholes with contrasting bias binding. Instructions on page 112.

9 Turn up a 3cm hem and finish it with matching bias binding. Instructions on page 116.

Pinafore Dress
from Crimplene Skirt

Sizes 2 (3, 4)

The little pinafore shown on page 30 is long enough to be worn as a dress on its own or, with the skirt shortened by 8cm, it would be equally useful over trousers. The bodice is fully lined, which avoids the trouble of facings at neck and armhole and, at the same time, gives the dress enough body to be made up from a cotton or polyester summer skirt.

Drafting the pattern

The back bodice

Cut a rectangle of paper 23 (23.5, 24) cm long by 19 (19.5, 20) cm wide, as in *figure 28*
Mark A at the top left-hand corner
A – B, down the left-hand edge, is 6.5

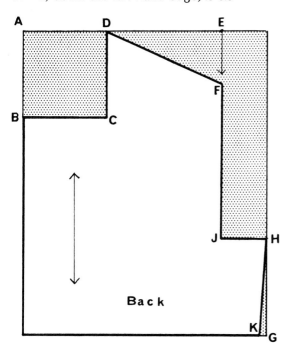

Figure 28

4 Pinafore dress from crimplene skirt

C is 6.5 to the right of B
Measuring along the top edge:
A – D is 6.5
D – E is 9 (9.5, 10)

F is 4 below E
Mark G at the bottom right-hand corner
H is 7.5 above G
J is 3.5 to the left of H
K is 0.5 to the left of G
Join B – C – D for the neckline
Join D – F for the shoulder seam
Join F – J – H for the armhole
Join H – K for the side seam
Cut out, discarding the shaded areas
Mark a straight-grain arrow down the pattern

The front bodice

Cut a rectangle of paper 22.5 (23, 23.5) cm long by 17 (17.5, 18) cm
wide, as in *figure 29.*
Mark A at the top right-hand corner
A – B, down the right-hand edge, is 11.5
C is 4.5 to the left of B
Measuring across the top edge:
A – D is 4.5
D – E is 9 (9.5, 10)

F is 3.5 below E
Mark G at the bottom right-hand corner
H is 5 to the left of G

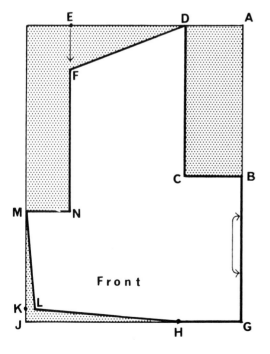

Figure 29

31

Mark J at the bottom left-hand corner
K is 1 above J
L is 0.5 to the right of K
M is 7.5 above K
N is 3.5 to the right of M
Join B – C – D for the neckline
Join D – F for the shoulder seam
Join F – N – M for the armhole
Join M – L for the side seam
Join L – H for the waistline
Cut out, discarding the shaded areas
Mark a fold-arrow down the right-hand side

The skirt

No paper pattern is needed for the skirt. It is a rectangle
38 (40, 43) cm long by at least 1 metre wide; in a thin fabric, you
could make it up to 1.5 metres wide if you have plenty of
material.

Cutting out

The layout for your pattern pieces will depend entirely on the
shape of the garment from which you are cutting. The pinafore
in the photograph was made from a straight skirt with a pleat at
the back and front, so the pattern pieces could be placed as
shown in *figure 30*. You will need to cut two each of the bodice
front, right back and left back (pattern reversed).

Figure 30

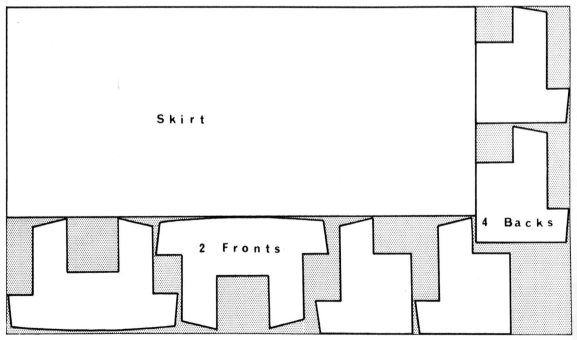

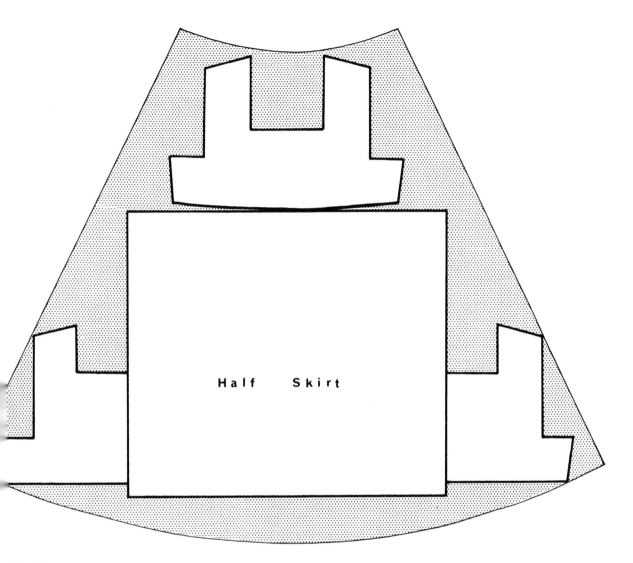

Figure 31

If however the skirt is flared, use a layout similar to the one shown in *figure 31*. Cut the front, two backs and half the skirt from the front of the adult skirt, and cut them again from the back. You will then need to make a seam down the centre-front of the pinafore skirt. If necessary, the skirt can be made from several panels seamed together.

Making up the pinafore

1 You will need 3 hooks and bars.
Seam allowance: 1.5cm. Hem allowance: 3cm.

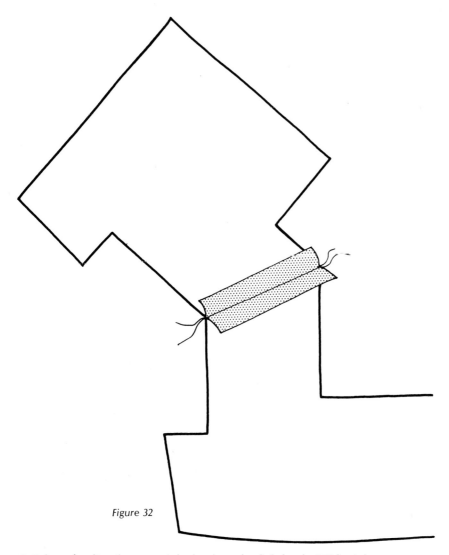

Figure 32

2 Take a bodice front, a right back and a left back. With right sides together, stitch the shoulder seams and press open the turnings *(figure 32)*.

3 Repeat with the remaining bodice pieces, for the lining.

4 Place bodice and lining with right sides together. Stitch round the neckline and back edges, beginning and finishing 1.5cm above the lower edge. You should stitch in a slight curve over the shoulders *(figure 33)*.

5 Stitch round both armholes, again making a curve over the shoulders. Do not stitch down the side seams.

6 Trim the seam turnings and clip into or across all corners.

7 Turn the bodice right-side-out by pushing each side of the back bodice through between the two thicknesses of fabric at the shoulder *(figure 34)*. Press.

8 Stitch the side seams of bodice and lining as one continuous seam *(figure 35)*.

9 If the skirt is cut in several panels, stitch the sections together. Stitch the centre-back seam, leaving 15cm open at the top. Press open the seam turnings.

10 Run gathering threads round the upper edge of the skirt. (Instructions for gathering are on page 113.)

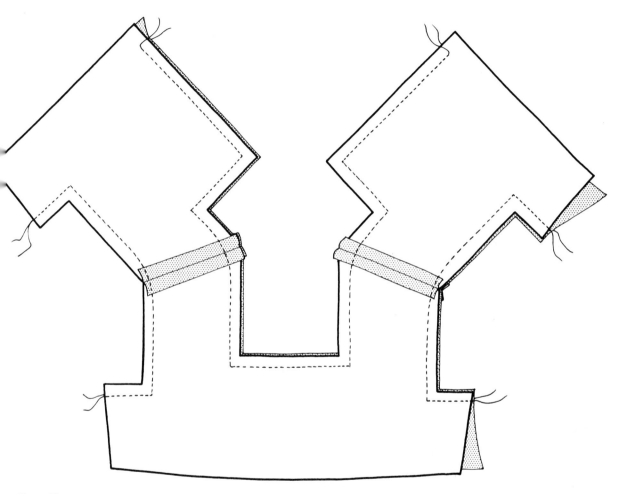

Figure 33

11 Pin the skirt to the bodice, right sides together, and pull up the gathers to fit. Stitch, being careful to keep the bodice lining out of the way *(figure 36)*.

12 Turn the lower edge of the bodice lining down behind the seam. Top-stitch from the right side along the seamline, to secure the lining *(figure 37)*.

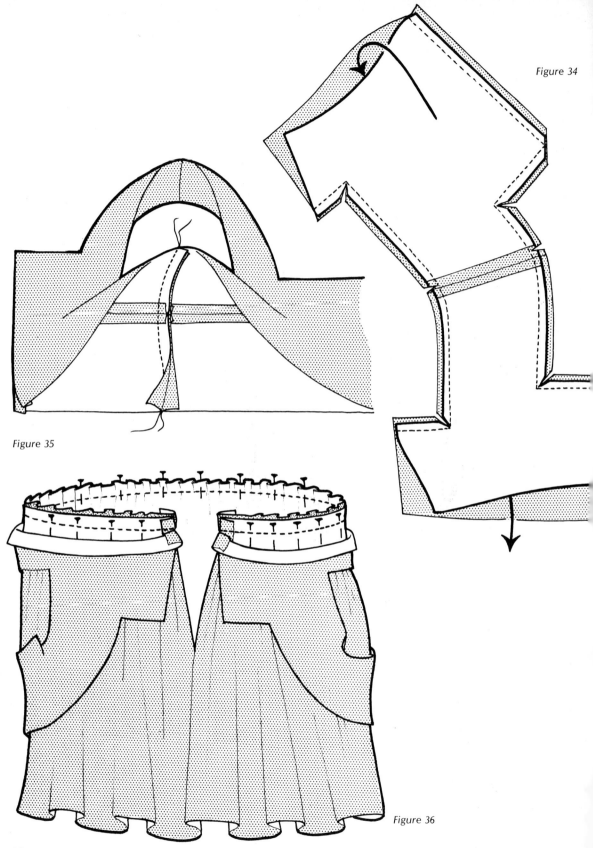

Figure 34

Figure 35

Figure 36

13 With a long stitch, and using buttonhole twist in the machine, top-stitch round the back opening and neckline, 1cm from the edge. Continue the top-stitching round the lower edge of the bodice *(figure 38)*.

14 Top-stitch round the armholes.

15 Inside the right bodice back, sew hooks at the neckline, the lower edge and midway between them. Overlap the right back 2cm over the left back, and sew on bars level with the hooks.

16 Turn up 3cm along the hemline and finish as shown on page 115. Top-stitch, if wished, to match the bodice.

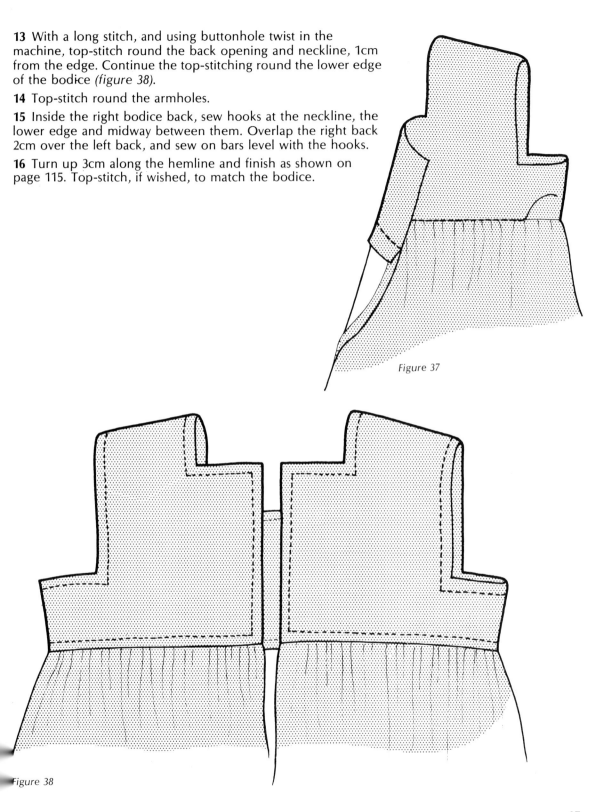

Figure 37

Figure 38

Bib-fronted Pants
from Tweed Skirt

Sizes 2 (3, 4)

The pants, shown on page 42, are very easy to make. The adjustable straps and elasticated waist allow plenty of room for growth. Decorative press studs fasten the straps, and there is extra strap length at the back, where it can be let out as needed.

Drafting the pattern

Back and front

Cut a rectangle of paper 47 (48, 49) cm wide by 29.5 (31.5, 33.5) cm long
Mark the corners A, B, C, D, as in *figure 39*.
Measuring down the left-hand edge:
A – E is 13.5 (14, 14.5)
A – F is 21 (22, 23)
G is 8 to the right of A, along the top edge

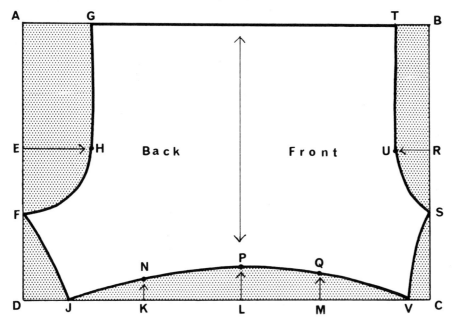

Figure 39

H is 8 to the right of E
Measuring along the bottom edge:
D – J is 5
D – K is 14.5
D – L is 25.5 (26, 26.5)
D – M is 34 (35, 36)
N is 2.5 above K
P is 4 above L
Q is 3 above M

Measuring down the right-hand edge:
B – R is 13.5 (14, 14.5)
B – S is 20.5 (21.5, 22.5)
T is 4 to the left of B, along the top edge
U is 4 to the left of R
V is 2.5 to the left of C, along the bottom edge
Join G – H – F for the centre-back seam. (G – H is a straight line;
H – F is a quarter circle)
Join F – J and S – V for the inside leg seam. (Both lines are
slightly hollowed)
Join T – U – S for the centre-front seam. (T – U is a straight line;
U – S is well curved)
Join J – N – P – Q – V for the hemline
Cut out, discarding the shaded areas
Mark a straight-grain arrow up from P

The bib
20cm square, all sizes

The straps
50cm by 10cm, all sizes

Cutting out

If the pattern is too wide to fit on a single skirt panel, cut it in half
along the straight-grain arrow and add seam allowances to the
cut edges, as on page 110. The layout on both back and front of
the skirt could then be as shown in *figure 40*. Cut two backs/
fronts, two bibs and two straps.

Making up the pants

1 You will need 45cm of elastic 1cm wide, and 2 stud fasteners.
Seam allowance: 1.5cm. Hem allowance: 2.5cm.

2 Stitch the centre-back and centre-front seams. Trim the
turnings of the lower, curved ends of the seams to 0.5cm and
machine zig-zag the edges together. Press the upper seam
turnings open and zig-zag them separately (*figure 41*).

3 Stitch the inside leg seam as one continuous seam. Press open
and finish the turnings separately.

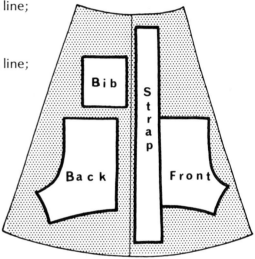

Figure 40

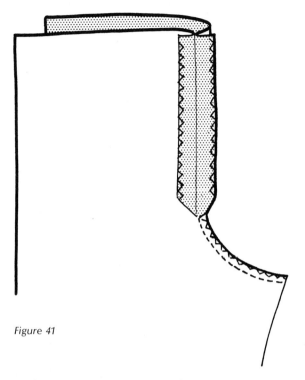

Figure 41

4 Place the two bib sections right sides together and stitch the side and top edges. Trim the seam allowances, turn and press.

5 Pin the bib to the centre-front of the pants, right sides together. Stitch 3cm from the edges *(figure 42)*. Finish the edges with zig-zag stitching all round.

6 Turn in 3cm round the waistline. Top-stitch close to the fold, and round the bib, as in *figure 43*.

7 Pin the elastic inside the casing, with the ends overlapping the sides of the bib *(figure 44)*. Fit to the child's waist. Machine as shown in *figure 45*, enclosing the elastic and securing its ends.

8 Fold each strap in half lengthwise; stitch 1cm from the edges and across one end. Turn and press.

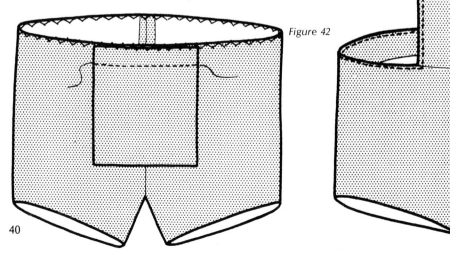

Figure 42

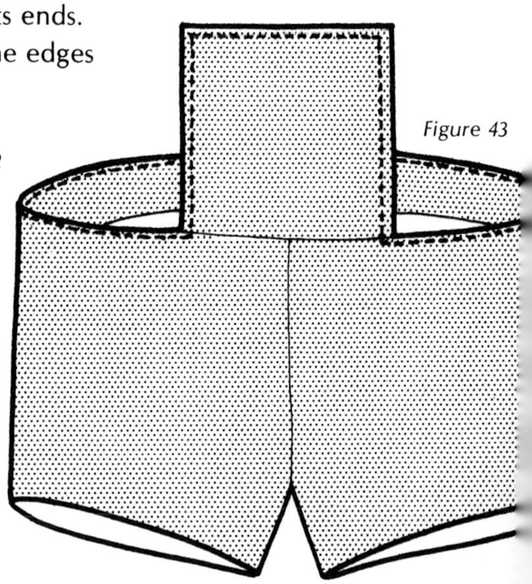

Figure 43

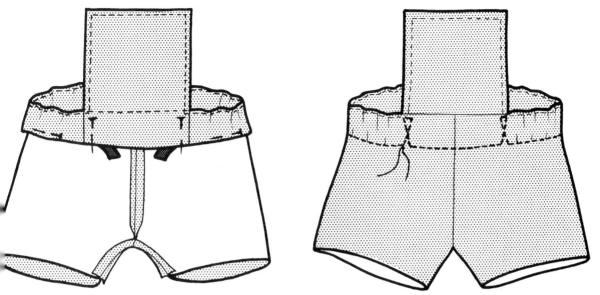

Figure 44

Figure 45

9 Apply the press studs to the corners of the bib and to the finished ends of the straps. Cross over the straps at the back and pin to the waistline, leaving the ends loose inside the pants. Try on for length. Machine in place as shown in *figure 46*. If you use a long machine stitch, it will be simple to pull out the stitching when you need to lengthen the pants.

10 Turn up the leg hems and finish as shown on page 115.

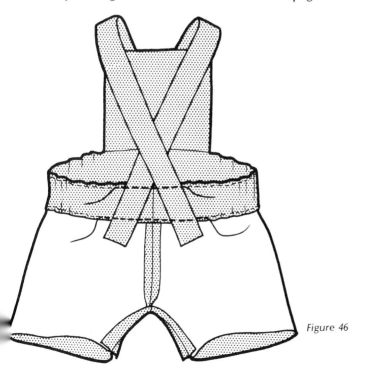

Figure 46

5 Bib-fronted pants from tweed skirt *(right)* and jeans from jeans

Jeans from Jeans

Sizes 5 (6, 7)

Well-worn and scruffy trousers may still be perfectly good on the wrong side of the fabric. The jeans shown on the left opposite were made up from the wrong side of denim, and actually retain the original side seam – a double-stitched seam that looked the same on both sides of the fabric.

The waist is fitted with elastic and there is no front opening; up to about size 7, this style gives a very reasonable fit and is easier for a child to manage.

Pockets are essential on jeans; here there are hip-pockets, but extra ones could be put on the front as well.

Drafting the pattern

Cut a rectangle of paper 70 (74, 78) cm long by 49.5 (51, 52.5) cm wide
Mark the corners A, B, C, D as shown in *figure 47*.
Measuring down the left-hand side:
A – E is 16.5 (17.5, 18)
A – F is 25.5 (26.5, 27.5)
A – G is 43 (46, 48)

H is 9.5 to the right of A, along the top edge
J is 8 to the right of E
K is 5.5 (5.5, 6) to the right of G
L is 5.5 (5.5, 6) to the right of D, along the bottom edge
M is 4 (4.5, 4.5) to the left of B, along the top edge
N is 1.5 below M
Measuring down the right-hand side:
B – P is 16.5 (17.5, 18)
B – Q is 25 (26, 27)
B – R is 43 (46, 48)

S is 4 (4.5, 4.5) to the left of P
T is 3 (3.5, 3.5) to the left of R
U is 3 (3.5, 3.5) to the left of C, along the bottom edge
Join H – N for the waistline
Join H – J – F for the centre-back seam. (H – J is a straight line; J – F is almost a quarter circle)
Join F – K – L for the inside leg seam. (F – K is gently curved; K – L is a straight line)

43

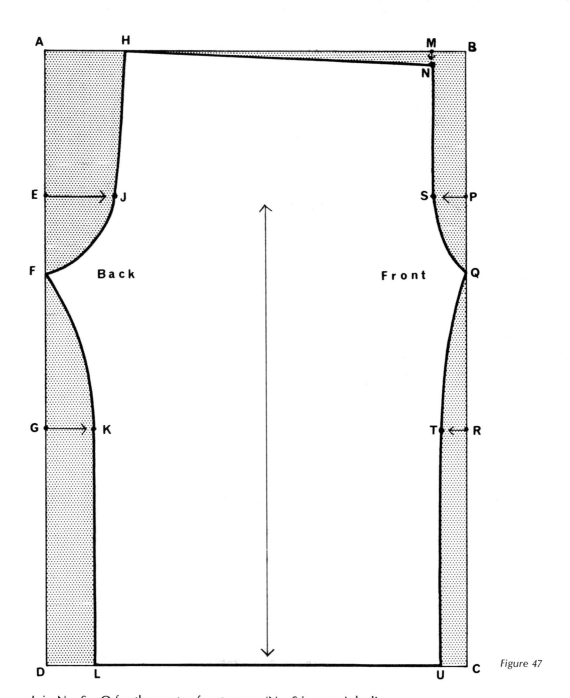

Figure 47

Join N – S – Q for the centre-front seam. (N – S is a straight line;
S – Q is gently curved)
Join Q – T – U for the inside leg seam. (Q – T is slightly curved;
T – U is a straight line)
Cut out, discarding the shaded areas
Mark a straight-grain arrow exactly down the centre of the leg;
this is easily done by folding K over to T, and L over to U, and
creasing. Mark the arrow down the crease.
Pockets are 13.5cm long by 12cm wide

Cutting out

Open up the centre-front, centre-back and inside leg seams of the adult trousers. In French-cut trousers, where the side seam is on the straight grain from the hip downwards, you should match the grain-arrow of the pattern to this seam, and cut the whole pattern in one piece. You will then retain the side seam in the child's jeans, see *figure 48*. (Turn over the pattern to cut the second leg.)

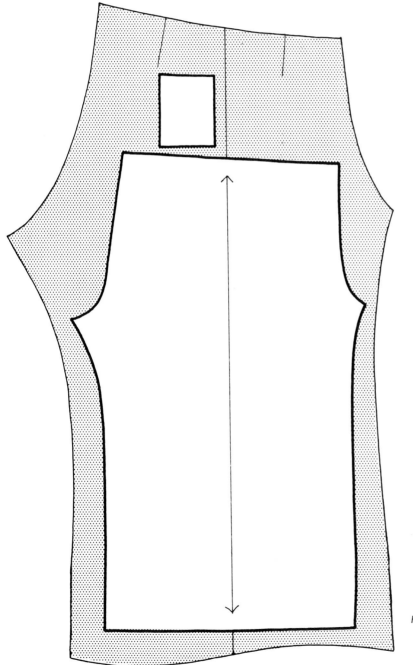

Figure 48

If however the side seam is shaped, you will have to cut your pattern from top to bottom down the grain-arrow, separate the halves and add a seam allowance (as shown on page 110) to each cut edge. Cut the back and front from the adult trouser leg as shown in *figure 49*. Turn over the patterns before cutting the second back and front.

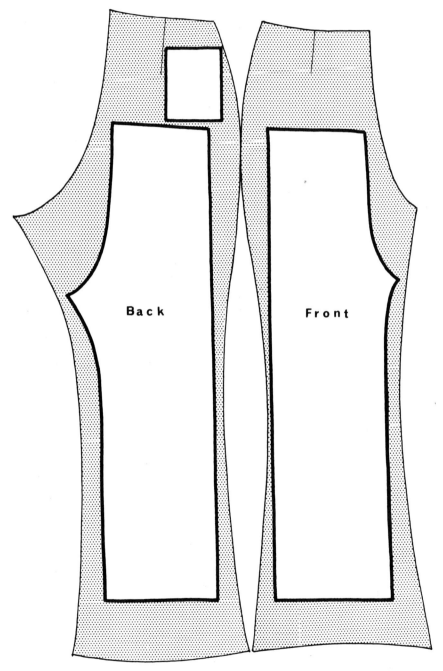

Back

Front

Figure 49

Making up the jeans

1 You will need 60cm of elastic 1cm wide. Also brads or studs to decorate the pockets, if liked.
Seam allowance: 1.5cm   (Pocket 1cm only.)
Hem allowance: 3cm   (Pocket 2.5cm.)

2 The side, centre-back and centre-front seams of jeans are usually double-stitched, as shown in *figure 50*. With wrong sides together, stitch the seam from the right side. Press the edges towards the front of the garment (in the case of centre seams, to the right). Trim the underneath seam-turning to half its width, fold in the edge of the other seam-turning under it, and top-stitch along the fold.

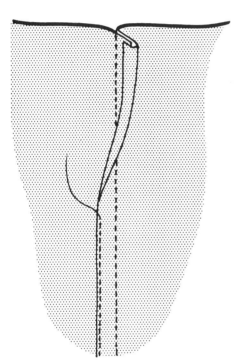

Figure 50

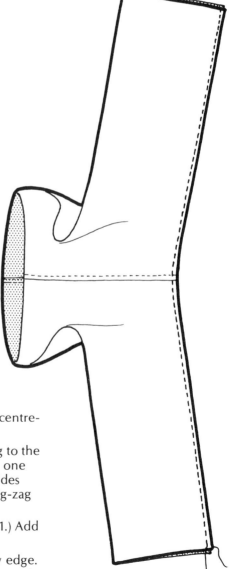

3 Stitch the side seams, if necessary, first. Then stitch the centre-back and centre-front seams.

4 Stitch the inside leg seam up from the bottom of the leg to the crutch and then down to the bottom of the other leg, in one continuous seam *(figure 51)*. Sew this seam with wrong sides together, press the seam turnings open and finish with zig-zag machine stitching.

5 Make the pockets as shown in *figures 19* and *20* (page 21.) Add any decoration of top-stitching at this stage.

6 Finish the waistline with zig-zag stitching along the raw edge. Turn in 3cm to make a casing for the elastic. Machine as shown in

Figure 51

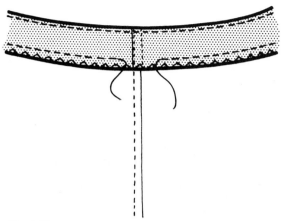

Figure 52

figure 52, leaving a short gap at the centre-back. Thread in the elastic.

7 Try on the jeans. Fit the elastic to the child's waist. Pin on the pockets where they look best.

8 Pin up the hems; trousers look better if the hemline is raised 0.5cm in front and dropped 0.5cm at the back. Trim the hem turnings to an even 2.5cm.

9 Finish the hems as shown on page 115.

10 Top-stitch the pockets in place.

Jersey Poncho
from Sweater

Sizes 2 (3, 4, 5, 6, 7)
Modelled by the smallest girl photographed on page 50, this
comfortable little cover-up could hardly be simpler to make. The
pattern can be adjusted for any child's size, the only limitation
being the amount of material available from the good parts of
the sweater. Sizes 2-4 can be made from a woman's jersey, but a
man's would probably be needed for the larger sizes. A jacquard
jersey, as here, or an Arran or fisherman's knit sweater would be
suitable.

Drafting the pattern

Cut a rectangle of paper 37 (38, 39, 40, 41, 42) cm square
Mark the corners A, B, C, D as shown in *figure 53*.
Crease diagonally from A to C
A – E along the top edge is 10cm for sizes 2-4; 11cm for sizes 5-7
A – F along the crease is the same length
A – G down the left-hand edge is the same length
C – H along the crease from the bottom right-hand corner is
12cm in all sizes

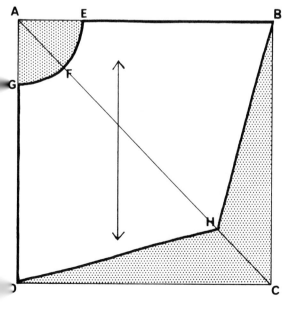

Figure 53

6 Cape from tweed skirt *(left)*, patchwork poncho *(centre)*, and jersey poncho from sweater

Join E – F – G in a quarter circle for the neckline
Join B – H – D for the hemline
Cut out, discarding the shaded areas
Mark a straight-grain arrow parallel to the left-hand edge

Cutting out

Cut the back and front of the poncho from the back and front of the sweater. The grain-arrow can run either across or down the sweater *(figure 54).*

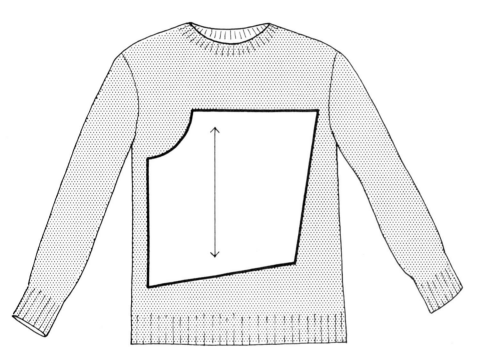

Figure 54

Making up the poncho

1 You will need 33cm of elastic trim 5cm wide for the neckline (35cm for the three larger sizes), thick wool, unravelled from the sweater, for the fringe.
Seam allowance: 1cm. Hem allowance: 1.5cm.
2 Set the machine to a medium zig-zag stitch. Stitch the two shoulder seams, and press open. Finish the seam turnings separately with a narrow zig-zag stitch, set in from the edge to avoid tangling and stretching. Try on, to make sure the neckline is big enough.
3 Seam together the ends of the neckline trim. With right sides together, stitch the trim to the neckline with a medium zig-zag, stretching the seam well as you stitch *(figure 55).*

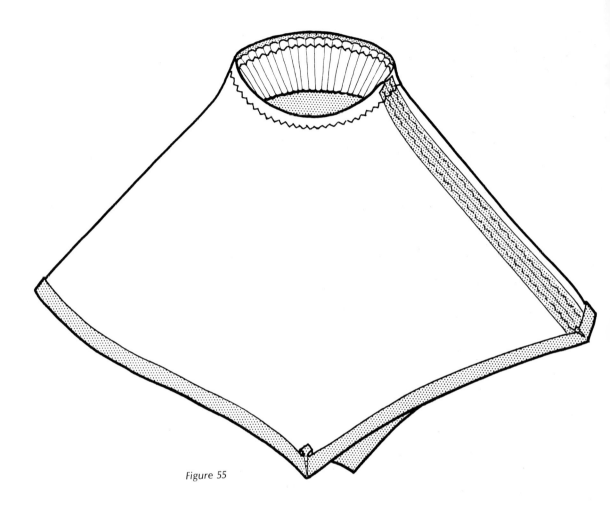

Figure 55

4 Press up the hem all round.

5 For the fringe, cut lengths of wool 20cm long. Knot them
1-1.5cm apart round the hem, through both thicknesses of
fabric, using four strands for each knot.

Cape from Tweed Skirt

Sizes 6 (7, 8, 9, 10, 11)

If you have a tweed skirt that is unfashionably short – preferably a flared one made in four gores – it can have a second life as a popover cape like the one shown on the left on page 50.

You do not even need a pattern for this one. You simply model the cape on your child's shoulders. The existing hem becomes the hem of the cape, where it will give plenty of width. In the smaller sizes, the hem can be brought to knee level, but in the larger sizes it will come above the knee.

This pattern is not really suitable for sizes below 6 because the skirt would need more extensive remaking, and also because a smaller girl, more likely to tumble over, might not be able to get her hands out quickly.

1 Cut off the whole waist finish.

2 Take out the zip and stitch up the seam opening.

3 Turn the skirt inside-out. Put it over the child's head, arranging two seams to come at the side-fronts. Pin shoulder seams to fit the child, and continue them, angled downwards, into long darts down the sides. Taper away to nothing to give a smooth line *(figure 56)*.

4 Now cut the neckline, scooped a little lower in front than at the back. Be sure to make the head opening big enough; children's heads are almost as large as adults', and a woven fabric will not oblige, as jersey does, by stretching.

5 Stitch the two seams, trim, press open and finish the edges with zig-zag stitching.

6 For a collar, cut the ribbed polo neck off an old sweater. If it is at all worn, use the reverse of the ribbing. Stitch the collar round the neckline, taking 1cm turnings, as in *figure 55*.

7 Open up two seams for the hand slits, at least 15cm long, at the level that suits the child. Finish by top-stitching all round, 1cm from the slits *(figure 57)*.

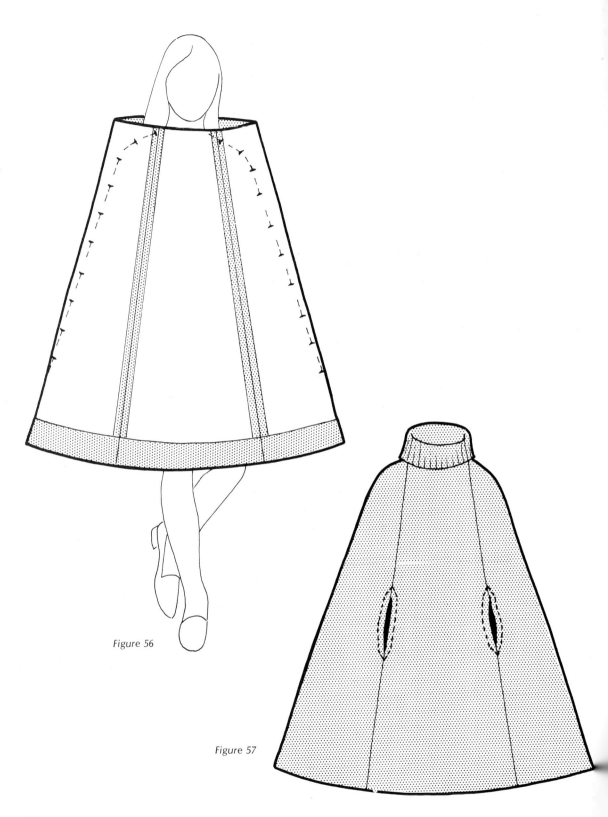

Figure 56

Figure 57

Patchwork Poncho

One size, to fit size 9 up to the Young Junior/Teen sizes.

Squares of several materials – the greater the variety the better – could be used for the poncho modelled by the eldest girl on page 50. This one was made from an old tweed jacket and scraps of leather and suède. It is not a garment that can be run up in a couple of hours, like the cape, as the lacing and fringing take a good deal of time; but otherwise it is very easy to make.

Drafting the pattern

The squares

The leather or suède patches are 18cm square. The fabric patches are 21cm square, to allow for turnings. The back and front of the poncho are the same, each taking eight squares *(figure 58)*.

The collar

Cut a rectangle of paper 67cm wide by 43cm long. Mark the top left-hand corner A and the bottom right-hand corner B, as in *figure 59*.
A – C, along the top edge, is 25

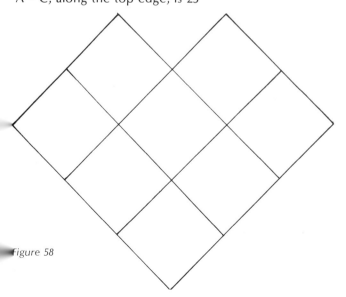

Figure 58

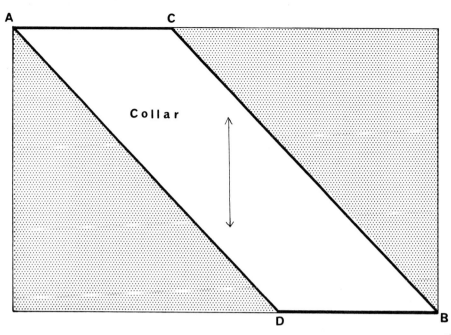

A   C

Collar

Figure 59

D   B

B – D, along the bottom edge, is 25
Join A – D and B – C
Cut out, discarding the shaded areas
Mark a straight-grain arrow as shown

Cutting out

Cut the fabric patches along the grain of the fabric. Cut leather or suède at any angle, fitting in the squares as economically as possible.

The collar will probably have to be made up from several pieces; seam them together along the straight grain, parallel to the grain-arrow of the pattern.

Making up the poncho

1 You will need 6 pairs of old nylon tights for the lacing and fringing.
Seam and hem allowances: Fabric – 1.5cm
                          Leather – None

2 Prepare the lengths of lacing from the tights by cutting the legs in spiral fashion to get one continuous strip, 3-4cm wide, from each leg. Pull out the strips to make them as long as possible. They will roll into fat cords as you stretch them. Each leg will make about 5 metres of cord *(figure 60)*.

3 On the fabric squares, fold the turnings to the wrong side and press *(figure 61)*.

4 You will need to make holes with a leather punch round the sides of the squares, to take the lacing. Mark off the positions first, 1.5cm apart. There should be 12 holes along each side. On leather, punch a medium-sized hole; on fabric, punch the

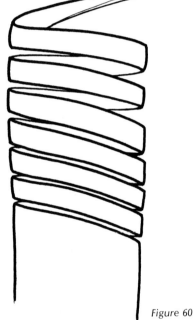

Figure 60

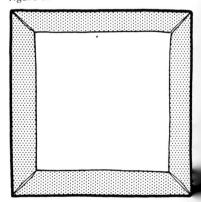

Figure 61

smallest-sized hole, through both thicknesses. Do not punch the neck and shoulder edges of the four squares that will go round the neckline.

5 Thread a lacing cord into a bodkin. Begin lacing the squares together with feather-stitching *(figure 62)*. When turning a corner, work twice into the last hole, as it is also the first hole of the next side. Make up the front and back separately.

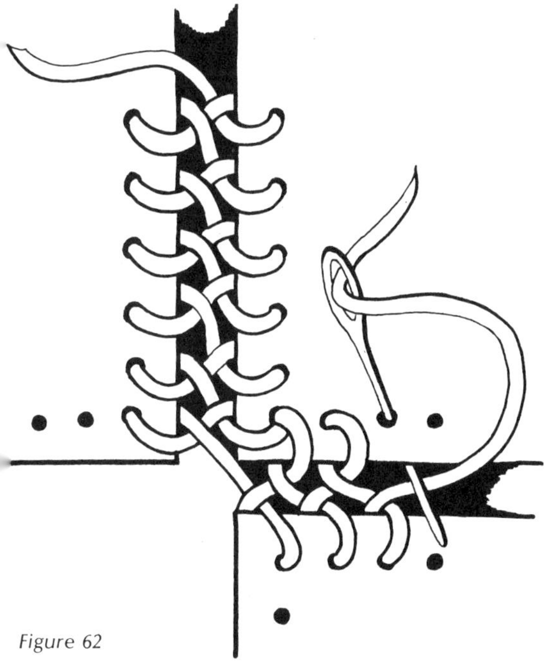

Figure 62

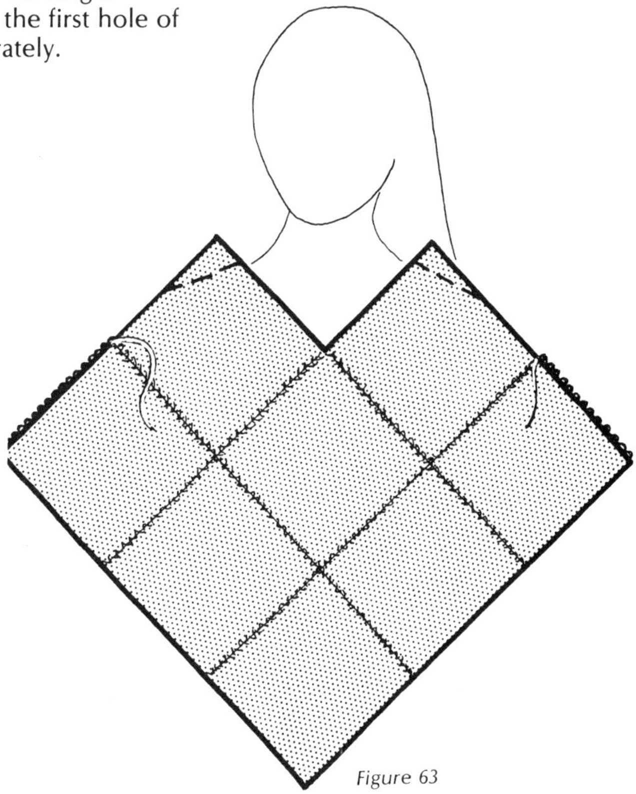

Figure 63

6 Lace together the lower halves of the side seams. Try on the poncho, mark the shaping for the shoulder as in *figure 63*, and trim as necessary. The narrow wedge you should trim off is unlikely to be wider than 3cm, or longer than 7cm in the smaller sizes; in the larger sizes, it might be up to 10cm long.

7 Punch the remaining holes along the trimmed shoulderline and complete the seams. Sew in all ends of the lacing cord on the wrong side.

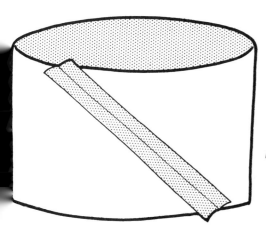

Figure 64

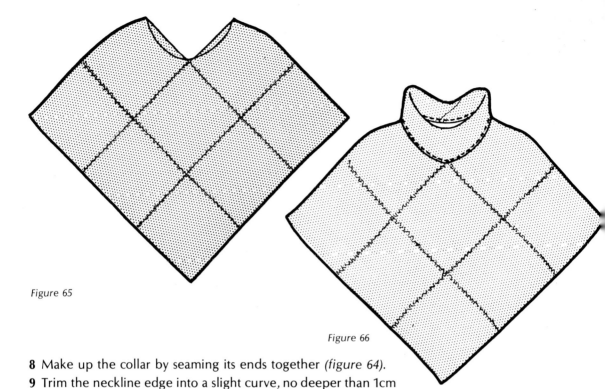

Figure 65

Figure 66

8 Make up the collar by seaming its ends together *(figure 64)*.

9 Trim the neckline edge into a slight curve, no deeper than 1cm at the centre of each neckline patch *(figure 65)*. With right sides together, stitch the collar to the neckline all round. Finish the free edge of the collar with zig-zag stitching, turn it to the inside and secure it by top-stitching from the right side, 0.5cm above the first stitching *(figure 66)*.

10 For the fringe, cut 156 lengths of the lacing cord, each 20cm long. If you do not have enough tights of one colour, a mixed fringe using several shades would look well. Knot once into each hole; put an extra knot where the squares join; and knot three times into the points at centre-front and centre-back. Finish the fringe by knotting the end of each strand *(figure 67)*.

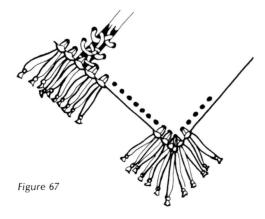

Figure 67

58

Pullover from Sweater

Sizes 5 (6, 7)

Hand-knitted woollies can easily be re-knitted for children, but machine-knitting may resist unravelling and in any case the yarn is usually too fine for re-knitting. It is better to treat the old sweater like a fabric, and cut the new garment from it. The pull-over shown on page 60 has an easy fit, with enough room for another jersey underneath.

The pattern is designed to use the good remaining parts of a sweater that may have worn elsewhere – under the arms or at the elbows. It is extremely easy to draft and make up. Remember, though, that all these knitted fabrics stretch and ravel abominably, so handle the pieces gently.

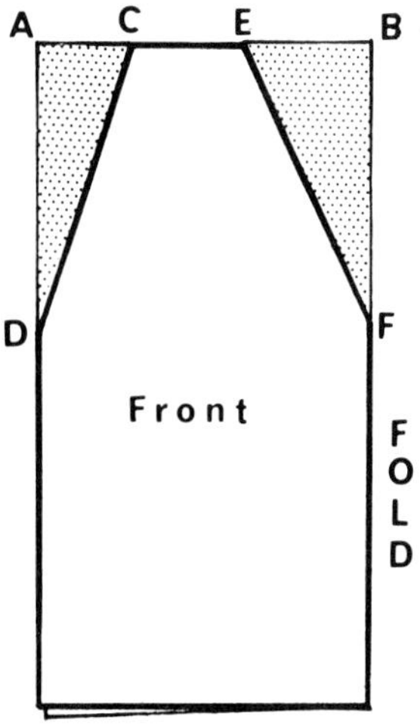

Drafting the pattern

The front

Cut a rectangle of paper 35 (36, 37) cm wide by 33.5 (35, 36) cm long. Crease it in half lengthwise, making it 17.5 (18, 18.5) cm wide, and put the fold at the right-hand side *(figure 68)*.
Mark the top left-hand corner A and the top right-hand corner B
A – C along the top edge is 5
A – D down the left-hand edge is 15
B – E along the top edge is 7
B – F down the right-hand fold is 14
Join C – D for the armhole
Join E – F for the V neckline
Cut out through both thicknesses, discard the shaded areas and unfold the pattern
Mark a straight-grain arrow down the crease

The back

Cut to the same measurements as the front. Omit the V neckline E – F, as the back is not shaped down

The sleeves

Cut a rectangle of paper 25cm wide by 36.5 (39, 41.5) cm long
Fold it in half lengthwise, to make it 12.5cm wide, and put the fold at the right-hand side *(figure 69)*.

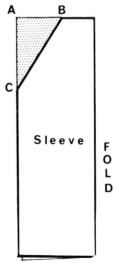

Figure 68

Figure 69

7 Pullover from sweater

Mark A at the top left-hand corner
A – B along the top edge is 7
A – C down the left-hand edge is 11
Join B – C for the sleevehead shaping
Cut out through both thicknesses, discarding the shaded area, and unfold the pattern
Mark a straight-grain arrow down the crease

Cutting out

Cut off the ribbing at neckline and waist, keeping the pieces intact. Cut open all the sweater seams and press the pieces to restore their shape. Cut the front, back and sleeves from their counterparts *(figure 70)*. For the neckline, cut a strip of ribbing 4cm wide by 44cm long. For the waistline, cut a strip of ribbing 5cm wide by 60 (62, 64) cm long.

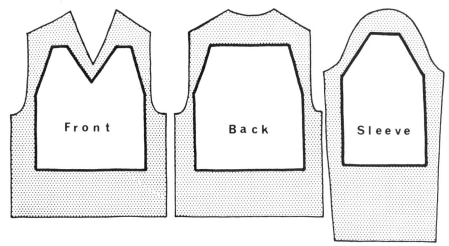

Figure 70

Making up the pullover

1 Seam allowance: 1cm. For all seams, use a long zig-zag stitch of medium width. Ease the fabric through the machine, being careful not to stretch it. Finish all seams by stitching the turnings together with a wide zig-zag stitch 0.5cm outside the seamline; then trim to this stitching. (Do not try to stitch along a cut edge of the knitting; it will get tangled down into the machine.)

2 Stitch a scant 1cm from the edges of the front V neckline, to prevent stretching *(figure 71)*.

3 Stitch and finish the shoulder seams, matching front and back at the armhole ends.

4 Stitch and finish the side seams.

5 Stitch the sleeve seams. Turn up 3cm at the wrist ends and machine the hem close to the raw edge. Machine again 0.5cm below this stitching.

6 Set in the sleeves as shown on page 117. (Gathering will not be necessary.)

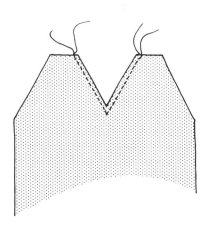

Figure 71

7 Centre the cut edge of the neckline ribbing to the centre-back neckline, right sides together. Stitch one side from centre-back down to the point of the V neckline *(figure 72)*. Stitch down the other side, meeting at the point.

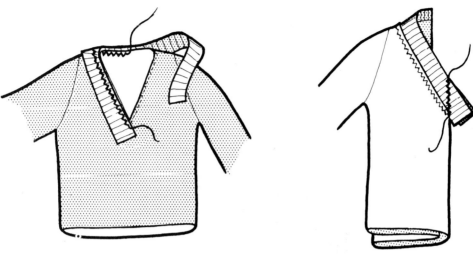

Figure 72

Figure 73

8 Press the ribbing up towards the neck. Turn the sweater inside-out and fold it down the centre-front. Stitch the ends of the ribbing as shown in *figure 73*, straight upwards from the point of the V. Press open these edges, trim and finish them separately.

9 Seam together the ends of the waistline ribbing. Seam the cut edge of the ribbing all round the waist edge of the pullover, stretching it slightly to fit.

Party Frock from Summer Dress

Sizes 2 (3, 4)

This is a traditional pattern for a small girl's party frock, with broderie anglaise frills at the neckline and sleeves. It would look pretty in any thin or silky fabric, or it could be made up in a fine wool mixture such as Viyella. The frock shown on page 64 could be cut from a sleeveless summer dress.

Drafting the pattern

The back bodice

Cut a rectangle of paper 26.5 (27.5, 28.5) cm long by 20.5 (21, 21.5) cm wide
Mark the corners A, B and C as shown in *figure 74*.
Measuring down the left-hand edge, A – D is 3
E is 6 to the right of D
Measuring from A along the top edge, A – F is 9
Measuring from B along the top edge, B – G is 3.5
H is 3.5 below G
Measuring down the right-hand edge:
B – J is 11
B – K is 15.5

L is 4 to the left of J
Measuring along the bottom edge, C – M is 1
Join D – E – F for the neckline. (D – E is a straight line; E – F is a quarter circle)
Join F – H for the shoulder seam
Join H – L – K for the armhole. (H – L is slightly hollowed; L – K is almost a quarter circle)
Join K – M for the side seam
Cut out, discarding the shaded areas
Mark a straight-grain arrow parallel to the left-hand edge

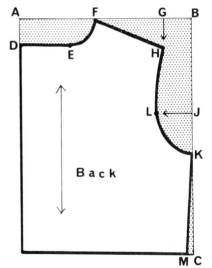

Figure 74

The front bodice

Cut a rectangle of paper 17 (17.5, 18) cm wide by 27 (28, 29) cm long
Mark the corners A, B, C, D as shown in *figure 75*.

8 Party frock from summer dress

Measuring down the left-hand edge:
A – E is 3
A – F is 9
A – G is 13.5

H is 3.5 to the right of E
J is 4.5 to the right of F
Measuring along the top edge: B – K is 5.5
Measuring down the right-hand edge:
B – L is 3
B – M is 6.5

N is 4.5 to the left of L
Measuring along the bottom edge:
C – P is 7.5
D – Q is 1.3

R is 2.3 above Q
Join G – J – H for the armhole. (G – J is a full curve;
J – H is a straight line)
Join H – K for the shoulder seam
Join K – N – M for the neckline. (K – N is a straight line;
N – M is almost a quarter circle)
Join G – R for the side seam
Join R – P for the waistline
Cut out, discarding the shaded areas
Mark a fold-arrow down the right-hand side

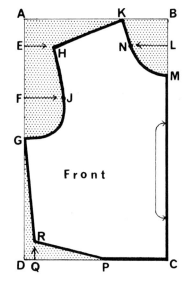

Figure 75

The sleeves

Cut a rectangle of paper 26 (26.5, 27) cm wide by 18cm long
Mark A at the top left-hand corner, as in *figure 76.*
Measuring down the left-hand edge:
A – B is 5
A – C is 10
Crease right across the pattern from B to D, and from C to E
Crease down the centre of the pattern, and mark F at the top of
the crease
G is 5 to the right of B
H is 5.5 to the left of D
Join C – G – F for the back of the sleevehead. (The curves flatten
out near C and F)
Join F – H – E for the front of the sleevehead. (H – E is almost a
quarter circle)
Cut out, discarding the shaded areas
Mark a straight-grain arrow down the crease from F

The skirt

The whole skirt is 140cm round, by 36 (38, 40) cm long

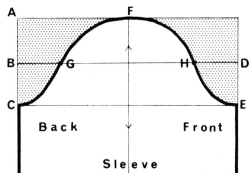

Figure 76

The pocket

10cm deep by 12cm wide, with the bottom corners rounded off

Cutting out

If you do not have a piece of fabric large enough to take the
skirt in one piece, cut it in as many sections as you need. It can be
narrower if necessary, but not less than 1 metre round. A possible
layout is shown in *figure 77*.

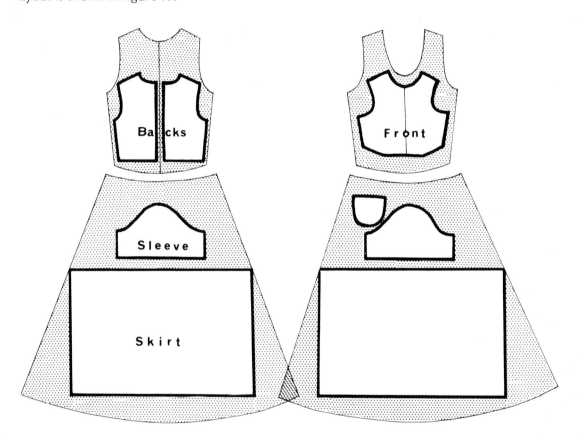

Figure 77

Making up the frock

1 You will need 1.2 metres of narrow broderie anglaise trimming
and 4 small buttons. Elastic thread for shirring.
Seam allowance: 1.5cm. Hem allowance: 3cm.

2 Stitch the bodice shoulder and side seams. Use French seams
as shown on page 113.

3 Fold in 0.5cm down each centre-back edge, and machine
along the fold. Turn in a further 2cm and press *(figure 78)*. Gather
50cm of broderie anglaise to fit the neckline and tack it to the

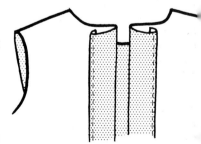

Figure 78

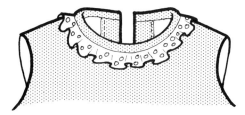

Figure 79

right side. Finish the neckline with bias binding *(figure 79)*. (Instructions on page 112.)

4 With right sides together, stitch broderie anglaise (ungathered) to each sleeve, 0.5cm from the edge. Press the turnings upwards and top-stitch. Wind the machine bobbin with elastic thread and work a line of machine stitching (longest stitch) 1cm above the previous stitching, to gather up the sleeve into a puffed shape *(figure 80)*.

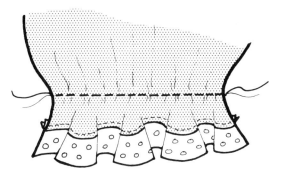

Figure 80

5 Work the sleeve seams as French seams; this will secure the ends of the elastic thread. Set the sleeves into the armholes as shown on page 117.

6 Stitch the skirt sections together in French seams. Stitch the centre-back seam, leaving open the top 12cm. This should be an ordinary flat seam, taking 2.5cm turnings; finish by turning the raw edges in 0.5cm and stitching.

7 Gather the upper edge of the skirt and stitch to the bodice. (Gathering instructions are on page 113.) Trim the seam and finish with zig-zag stitching *(figure 81)*. Top-stitch just above the seam.

8 Work evenly-spaced machine buttonholes (page 116) on the right back. Overlap the right back 2cm over the left and sew on buttons to correspond to the buttonholes.

9 Turn up the hem, fold in the raw edge and machine. On a fine fabric, you could finish the hem by hand as shown on page 114.

10 Press under 1cm round the sides and bottom of the pocket. Finish the top with gathered broderie anglaise and binding, as for the neckline. Top-stitch to the skirt at a level that suits the child.

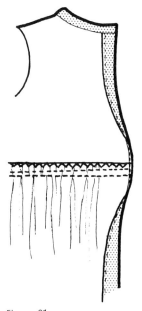

Figure 81

Long Party Dress
from Shirt-Dress

Sizes 5 (6, 7)

The dress shown opposite could be a little girl's first long party dress. It is in a dark, printed voile, with a raised waistline and with sleeves and neck finished quite plainly with binding, to set off the sheer, pale pink frilly pinafore.

Drafting the pattern

The back bodice

Cut a rectangle of paper 26.5 (28, 29) cm long by 19.5 (20, 20.5) cm wide
Mark its corners A, B, C as shown in *figure 82*.
A – D down the left-hand edge is 3
E is 4.5 to the right of D
A – F along the top edge is 7.5
Measuring down the right-hand edge:
B – G is 4
B – H is 12
B – J is 17

K is 3.5 to the left of G
L is 4.5 to the left of H
C – M along the bottom edge is 0.5
Join D – E – F for the neckline. (D – E is a straight line; E – F is a quarter circle)
Join F – K for the shoulder seam
Join K – L – J for the armhole. (K – L is slightly hollowed; L – J is almost a quarter circle)
Join J – M for the side seam
Cut out, discarding the shaded areas
Mark a straight-grain arrow parallel to the left-hand edge

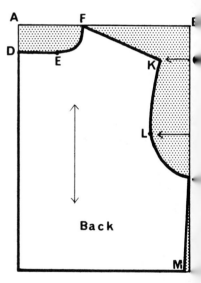

Figure 82

The front bodice

Cut a rectangle of paper 26 (27.5, 28.5) cm long by 18 (18.5, 19) cm wide
Mark its corners A, B, C, D as in *figure 83*
Measuring down the left-hand edge:
A – E is 3.5
A – F is 10
A – G is 15.5

68

9 Long party dress from shirt-dress with long pinafore from sheer nightdress

H is 3 to the right of E
J is 4.5 to the right of F
B – K along the top edge is 6
Measuring down the right-hand edge:
B – L is 3.5
B – M is 7

N is 5 to the left of L
C – P along the bottom edge is 7.5
D – Q along the bottom edge is 0.5
R is 1 above Q
Join G – J – H for the armhole. (G – J is almost a quarter circle;
J – H is a straight line)
Join H – K for the shoulder seam
Join K – N – M for the neckline. (K – N is a straight line)
Join G – R for the side seam
Join R – P for the waistline
Cut out, discarding the shaded areas
Mark a fold-arrow down the right-hand side

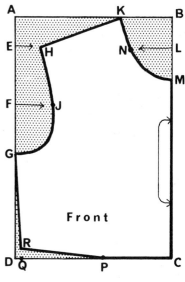

The sleeves

Figure 83

Cut a rectangle of paper 30 (31, 32) cm wide by 19.5 cm long
Mark the corners A, B, C as shown in *figure 84.*
Measuring down the left-hand edge:
A – D is 5.5
A – E is 11
Crease right across the pattern from D to F and from E to G
Crease down the centre of the pattern and mark the top of the
crease H
J is 5.5 to the right of D
K is 7 to the left of F
B – L up the left-hand edge is 1
B – M along the bottom edge is 8
C – N up the right-hand edge is 1
C – P along the bottom edge is 8

Join E – J – H for the back of the sleevehead
Join H – K – G for the front of the sleevehead. (K – G is almost a
quarter circle)
Join L – M and P – N for the hem edge
Cut out, discarding the shaded areas
Mark a straight-grain arrow down the pattern from H

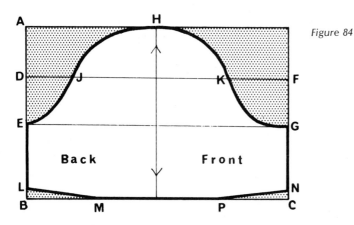

Figure 84

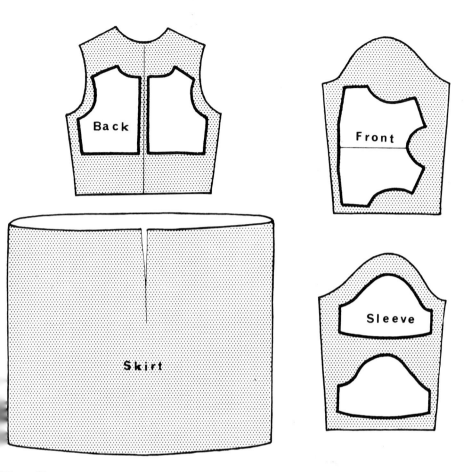

Figure 85

Cutting out

The dress on page 69 was made from a dress with a front opening; so the front bodice pieces were too narrow for the front pattern. If this happens to be your problem too, use a layout similar to the one in *figure 85*. The bodice front is cut lengthwise from one sleeve; in most fabrics, where there is no stripe or discernible direction in the print, this works perfectly well.

The whole of the old skirt can be used, retaining its seams and even its hem; the length is adjusted at the waistline edge, to leave a finished length of 66 (70, 75) cm. (The largest size is unlikely to need any trimming down.)

Making up the dress

Seam allowance: 1.5cm
You will need a 35cm zip.

Stitch the bodice shoulder and side seams as French seams (page 113).

3 Stitch the sleeve seams as French seams. Gather the lower edges of the sleeves to fit the child's arm, and finish with bias binding (instructions on page 112).

4 Set in the sleeves as shown on page 117.

5 Try on the bodice, inside out. Pin waistline darts at the front and back, if needed. Each one should not take up more than 1cm *(figure 86)*. Stitch and press.

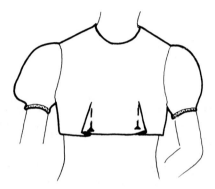

Figure 86

6 On the skirt, open up 14cm at the top of the centre-back seam. Gather the upper edge of the skirt to fit the bodice; tack and stitch the waistline seam. Instructions for gathering are on page 113.

7 Set in the back zip as shown on page 118.

8 Finish the neckline with bias binding, taking in the ends of the zipper tapes.

Long Pinafore
from Sheer Nightdress

Sizes 5 (6, 7)

This pale, frilly pinafore *(figure 87* and page 69) is designed to complement the dark print of the dress. Made from the sheer nylon tricot overskirt of a nightdress, it will allow the pattern of the dress fabric to show through. It will also, of course, mean that the seams will be totally visible, so they must all be very narrowly finished.

Figure 87

Drafting the pattern

The bodice

This is very simple. Pin the back and front dress bodice patterns together at the shoulder seam, overlapping the seam allowances. Place tracing paper (or greaseproof paper) over the pinned pattern, and draw in the neck and armhole lines of the pinafore, as in *figure 88*. As these are styling lines, they can be drawn as you wish. Here, the centre-front length of the bodice, below the neckline, is 14cm. The shoulder width should be not less than 4cm. The centre-back seam and the side seams are 6cm long; at the sides, they are set in 1cm from the dress bodice – at the centre-back, 2cm.

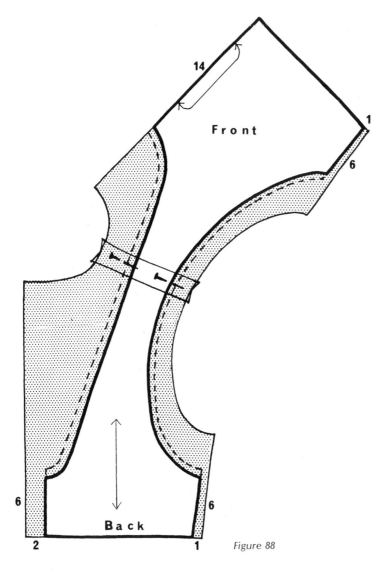

Figure 88

74

Now add 1cm seam allowances along the neck and armhole edges (shown here as broken lines), and cut out the pattern. Mark a fold-arrow at the centre-front and a straight-grain arrow down the back. Cut the pattern across at the shoulder seam and add a 1cm shoulder seam allowance to each piece.

The skirt, ties and frills

No patterns needed.

Cutting out

The skirt of the nightie will probably be about 90cm square, back and front. Lay out the fabric with a fold at the left-hand side. Arrange the pattern pieces as shown in *figure 89*.

The Skirt should be 55cm long at the centre-front, and at least 1.20 metres wide – or as wide as your fabric will allow. To give a graceful line, cut it in a curve up the back.
The Bodice Cut 2 fronts and 4 backs, as the bodice is lined.
The Waist Ties are 12cm wide and at least 80cm long.
The Frills for the armholes are 6cm wide and 90cm long.
The Flounce for the hemline is 8cm wide and 4 metres long.

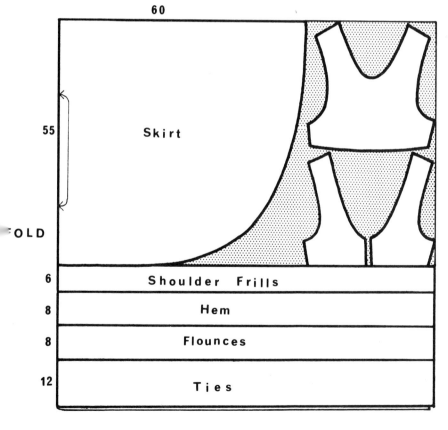

Figure 89

Making up the pinafore

1 Seam allowance: 1cm.

2 Seam together the sections of the hem flounce. Trim the turnings to 2mm. Finish one long edge with zig-zag stitching in a contrasting colour; a short stitch of medium width will give the prettiest effect – but try different stitch sizes first on a scrap of fabric. Hold the flounce tightly stretched out as you stitch, to frill out the edge *(figure 90)*.

3 Finish one edge of each shoulder frill in the same way.

4 Fold the waist ties in half lengthwise and stitch the long side and one end, machining the end to a point. Trim the seam turnings to 2mm, turn through to the right side and press.

5 Stitch the shoulder seams of bodice and lining. Press open and trim to 2mm wide.

6 Gather the unfinished edge of the shoulder frills (as shown on page 113), using the gathering threads to shape the ends to a point *(figure 91)*. Draw up the frills to make them 4cm shorter than the armholes. Pin them to the right side of the bodice as shown in *figure 92*. Pin the waist ties to the centre-back.

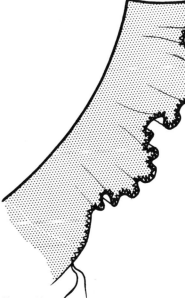

Figure 90

7 Lay the bodice lining right-side-down over the bodice and frills. Stitch the armhole seams. Stitch the centre-back and neck-line seams, taking in the ends of the waist ties. (Be careful not to catch any of the frilling in the neckline seam.) Trim all turnings to 2mm *(figure 93)*. Turn the bodice right-side-out by pushing the the two backs through the shoulders. Press.

8 Stitch the underarm seams of bodice and lining as one continuous seam. Trim to 2mm *(figure 94)*.

9 Gather the unfinished edge of the hem flounce. With right sides together, stitch it all round the curved edge of the skirt. Press the turnings upwards. Top-stitch and trim narrowly.

10 Gather the upper edge of the skirt to fit the bodice, and stitch with right sides together.

11 Turn the lower edge of the bodice lining down behind the waist seam. Secure it by top-stitching from the right side, immediately above the seam. If your machine has built-in embroidery stitches, use one of these for the top-stitching; here, the scallop stitch was used, with contrasting thread to match the frills.

Figure 91

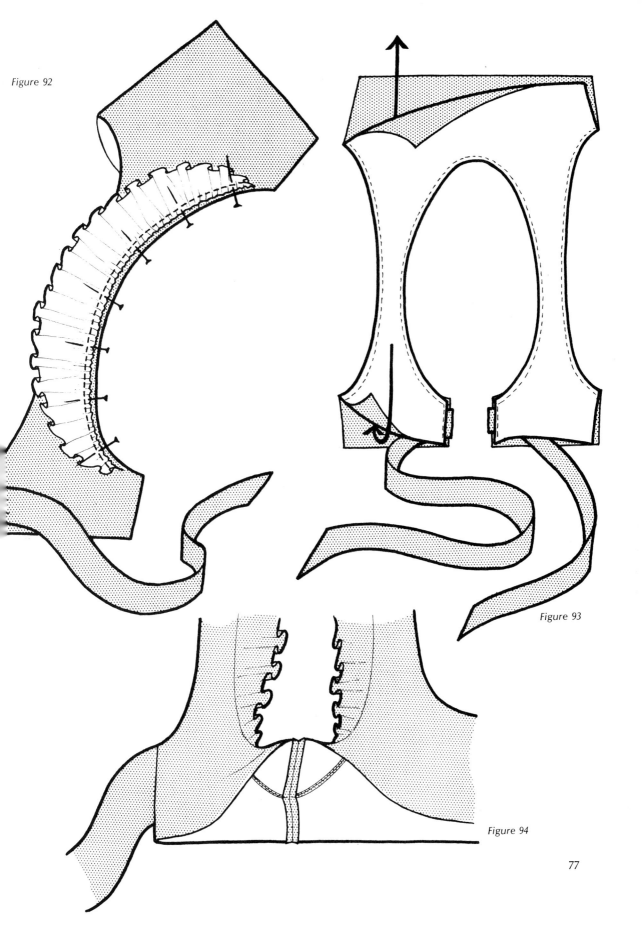

Figure 92

Figure 93

Figure 94

Quilted Pinafore Dress from Jersey Dress

Sizes 8 (9, 10, 11)

The pinafore dress shown opposite was made from a jersey dress that was too short, but widely-enough flared to give a girl's half-circular skirt.

The pattern is designed for a firm double-jersey; it would not be suitable for a very stretchable knit, as the skirt might drop unevenly. The quilted bodice and hem band give a festive air to this little dress.

Drafting the pattern

The back

Cut a rectangle of paper 33 (34, 35.5, 37) cm long by 13.5 cm wide
Mark the corners A, B and C as shown in *figure 95*.
A – D down the left-hand edge is 3
E is 5 to the right of D
A – F along the top edge is 8.5
Measuring down the right-hand edge:
B – G is 2
B – H is 16

J is 3.5 to the left of H
K is 4.5 to the left of C
Join D – E – F for the neckline. (D – E is a straight line; E – F is almost a quarter circle)
Join F – G for the shoulder seam
Join G – J – K for the side edge. (G – J is slightly hollowed; J – K is a straight line)
Cut out, discarding the shaded areas
Mark a straight-grain arrow parallel to the left-hand edge

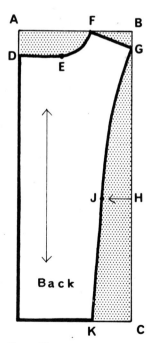

Figure 95

The front

Cut a rectangle of paper 35.5 (36.5, 38, 39.5) cm long by 12cm wide
Mark the corners A, B and C as shown in *figure 96*
Measuring down the left-hand edge, A – D is 2
A – E along the top edge is 5

10 Quilted pinafore dress from jersey dress

Measuring down the right-hand edge:
B – F is 12
B – G is 14
Measuring up the right-hand edge, C – H is 8.5
J is 3 to the left of F
K is 8.5 to the left of H
Join D – E for the shoulder seam
Join E – J – G for the neckline. (E – J is a straight line; J – G is
fully curved)
Join D – K – C for the side edge. (D – K is a straight line;
K – C is a quarter circle)
Cut out, discarding the shaded areas
Mark a fold-arrow down the right-hand edge

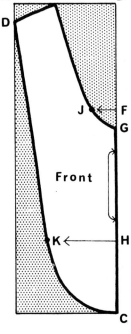

Figure 96

The skirt

Cut a square of paper with sides of 63 (66, 69.5, 72) cm.
Mark the corners A, B, C, D as shown in *figure 97*.
Place the end of a tape measure at A. Swing it round to mark out a
quarter-circle between E and F, of 19 (19, 20, 20) cm radius.
Still measuring from A, mark out a quarter-circle between
B and D.

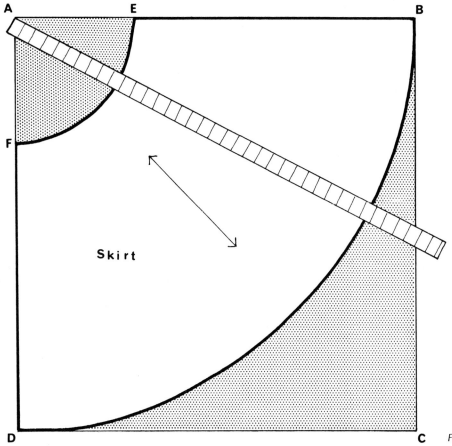

Figure 97

Cut out, discarding the shaded areas.
Mark a straight-grain arrow between A and C, diagonally across the pattern.

Cutting out

If you have too little fabric for a half-circular skirt, re-draw the lines E – B and F – D as shown in *figure 98* to give less hem width. Do not alter the waistline measurement E – F.

The back and front bodice pieces are cut from the dress bodice or sleeves. A suggested layout is shown in *figure 99*. Cut one skirt section in half, to give a centre-back seam.

When you have cut all the pieces in jersey fabric, trim a band 10cm wide from the hem edge of the skirt pattern, and use it as the pattern for the printed hem band. The printed bodice pieces are cut from the same pattern as the jersey ones.

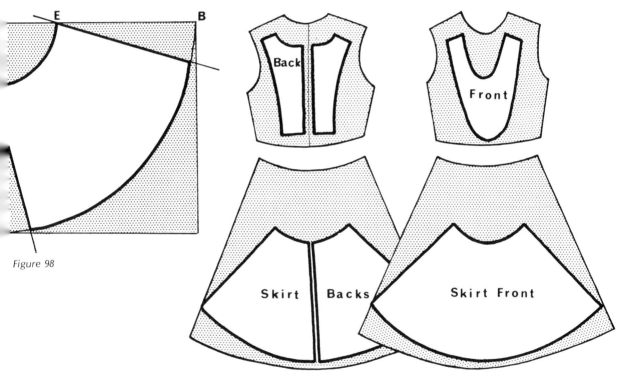

Figure 98

Figure 99

Making up the pinafore dress

1 Seam allowance: 1.5cm.
You will need a 40cm zipper, 60cm of elastic 1cm wide, and 2 metres of toning bias binding.

2 Stitch the shoulder seams of the bodice and jersey lining. Tack them with wrong sides together and mark out the quilting lines with tailor's chalk, pins or tacking. The quilting can be in

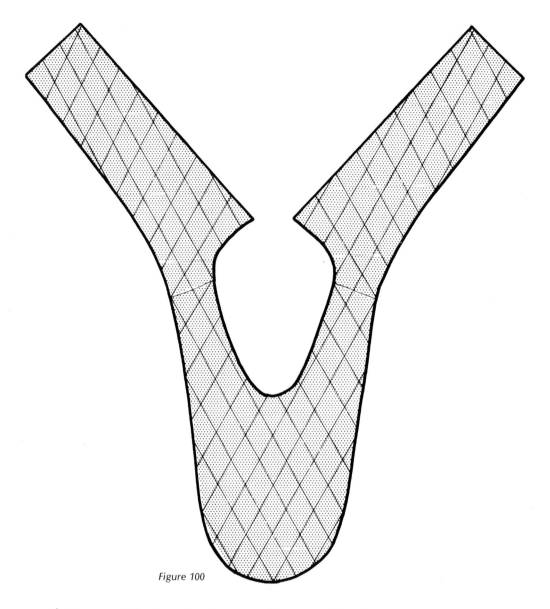

Figure 100

any design you wish; here, the lines were 5cm apart, forming diamond shapes *(figure 100)*. Make sure the design is centred down the front and back. Machine with a long stitch through both thicknesses, working all the lines in one direction first and then all the lines that cross them.

3 Bind the outer edge of the bodice, up one back, round the front and down the other back. (Instructions for bias binding are on page 112.)

4 Stitch the skirt side seams. Stitch the centre-back seam, leaving open the top 13cm.

5 Finish the upper edge of the skirt with elastic to fit the child's

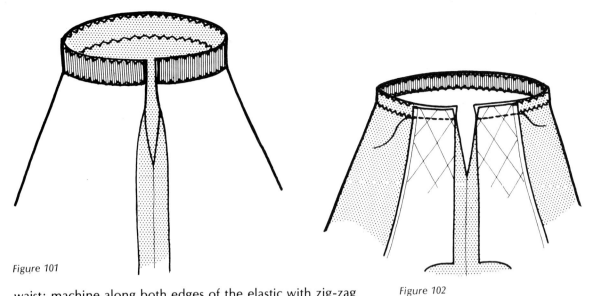

Figure 101

Figure 102

waist; machine along both edges of the elastic with zig-zag stitching, stretching it to fit the skirt *(figure 101)*.

6 With right sides together, stitch the back bodice sections to the skirt, matching the centre-back edges *(figure 102)*. Press the seams open, and fold the elastic waistband down to the inside.

7 Set in the zip, as shown on page 118.

8 Bind the neckline, taking in the top ends of the zipper tapes.

9 Seam together the sections of the hem band. With *right* side of band to *wrong* side of skirt, machine round the hemline. Turn the band over to the outside of the skirt, press in 1cm along the free edge, and top-stitch 3mm from the fold. Top-stitch the lower edge to match *(figure 103)*.

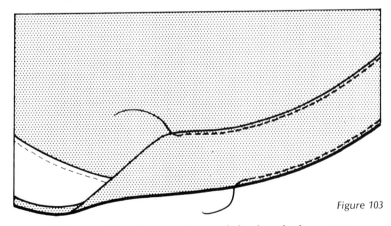

Figure 103

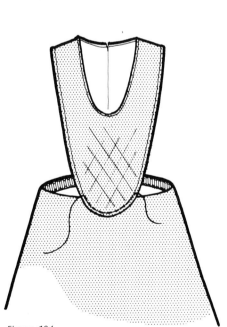

Figure 104

10 Work the quilting design all round the band. If you are working in diamond shapes, measure the finished width of the hemline and divide it into an exact number of repeats.

11 Try on the pinafore. Pin the lower edge of the bodice to the skirt at the centre-foot, overlapping them to fit the girl snugly – probably about 2cm. On the right side, machine in place round the inner edge of the binding. On the wrong side, hem the skirt edge to the bodice lining *(figure 104)*.

Magyar Overdress
from Contrasted Prints

Sizes 8 (9, 10, 11)

A single dressmaking remnant may not be large enough for a child's dress; but with some contrasting scraps, either printed or plain, you could make the overdress opposite. This lively style, trimmed with narrow braid, was designed to make use of quite small pieces of material.

Drafting the pattern

The bodice front

Cut a rectangle of paper 20 (21.5, 23, 25) cm wide by 22.5 (23.5, 25, 26.5) cm long
Mark its top corners A and B as shown in *figure 105*
A – C along the top edge is 8
B – D along the top edge is 8
E is 3.5 below C
F is 3.5 below D
G is at the centre of the lower edge
H is 4.5 above G
Join A – E – H – F – B for the neckline
Cut out, discarding the shaded area
Mark a straight-grain arrow down the pattern

The bodice back

The same size as the bodice front, but with no neckline shaping.

The sleeves

Cut a rectangle of paper 18cm wide by 42 (44, 47, 50) cm long
Fold it in half, with the fold along the top as in *figure 106*
Mark A at the bottom left-hand corner
A – B up the left-hand edge is 2.5
C is 3.5 to the right of B
A – D along the bottom edge is 6
Join B – C – D for the underarm shaping. (B – C is a straight line; C – D is a quarter circle)
Cut out, discard the shaded area and unfold the pattern
Mark a straight-grain arrow parallel to the right-hand edge

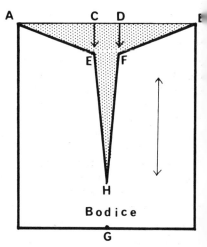

Figure 105

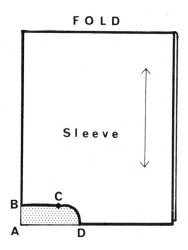

Figure 106

11 Magyar overdress from contrasted prints

Cutting out

No patterns are needed for the remaining dress pieces; they can be marked out with tailor's chalk directly on the fabric. Shorter lengths can be pieced together for the bands and waist ties.

The larger print is used for the sleeves, skirt and hem band *(figure 107).*

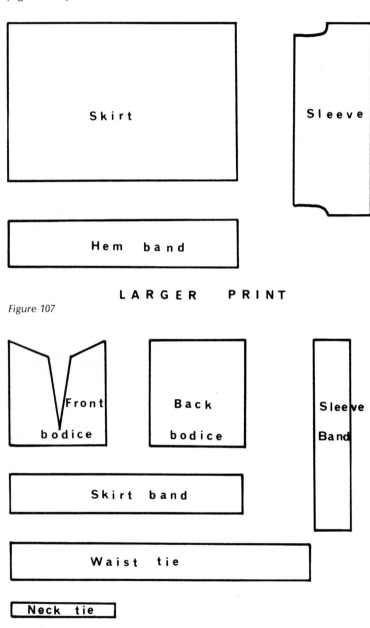

L A R G E R   P R I N T

Figure 107

S M A L L E R   P R I N T

Figure 108

Cut:
2 sleeves.
2 skirt pieces   55 (55, 60, 60) cm wide by 32 (35, 37.5, 40) cm long
2 hem bands   55 (55, 60, 60) cm wide by 18cm long.

The smaller print makes the bodice, ties and bands *(figure 108)*.

Cut:
2 bodice fronts (1 for the lining).
1 bodice back.
2 sleeve bands 42 (44, 47, 50) cm long by 10cm wide.
2 skirt bands 55 (55, 60, 60) cm long by 10cm wide.
2 waist ties 70cm long by 10cm wide.
2 neck ties 24cm long by 3cm wide.

Making up the overdress

1 Seam allowance: 1.5cm. You will need 4 metres of narrow 2-cord braid for trimming.

2 Make up the neck ties by folding them edges-to-middle (wrong sides together), then folding again and stitching *(figure 109)*.

Figure 109

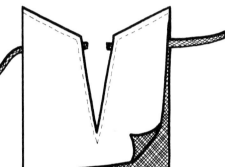

Figure 111

3 Fold the waist ties in half lengthwise and machine the long side and a pointed end. Turn through to the right side and press *(figure 110)*.

Figure 110

4 Seam together the front bodice and lining along the neckline, taking in the unfinished ends of the neck ties as shown in *figure 111*. Clip to the point of the stitching at the centre-front, turn through to the right side and press.

5 Machine a 1.5cm hem along the top edge of the back bodice.

6 Stitch the sleeve-bands to the sleeves. Stitch the braid over the seam *(figure 112)*.

7 Seam the sleeves to the back and front bodices, taking in the unfinished ends of the waist ties as in *figure 113*. Stitch braid over the seams.

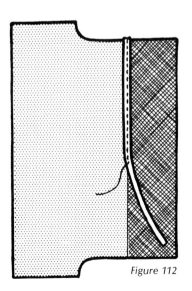

Figure 112

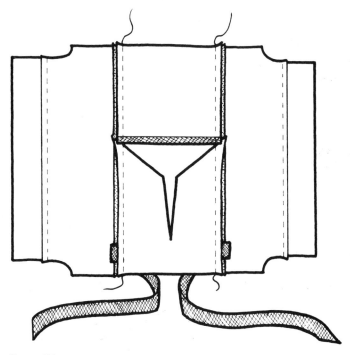

Figure 113

8 Stitch the sleeve underarm seams, clipping the turnings at the curve. Turn up and stitch a narrow hem to the sleeves *(figure 114).*

9 At the centre of the skirt front, make 7 tucks, 1cm wide and 9cm long, spaced 1cm apart *(figure 115).*

Figure 114

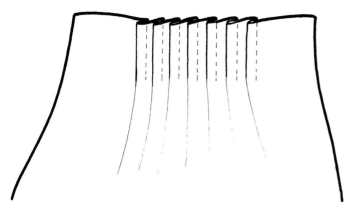

Figure 115

10 Assemble the back and front skirt and bands as shown in *(figure 116)*. Stitch braid over the horizontal seams. Lastly, stitch the remaining side seam.

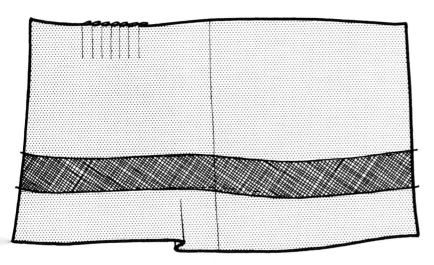

Figure 116

11 Gather the upper edge of the skirt to fit the bodice. Spread the gathers evenly all round, except across the tucks. Stitch to the bodice. (Instructions for gathering on page 113.)
12 Turn up and stitch the hem.

Shirred Dress
from Nightie

Sizes 8 (9, 10)

Nothing could be simpler than making the tube dress, shaped with elastic shirring, shown on the left opposite. This one was made from a polyester/cotton nightie – even the narrow lace trimming could be used again.

Cutting out

You do not need a pattern. Open up one skirt seam of the nightie and use its whole width, leaving any other seams intact; the shirring will provide the fit of the bodice. The dress should be cut 68 (72, 76) cm long; it consists of just one rectangular piece.

Cut two frills 55cm long by 8cm wide, and two shoulder straps 32cm long by 6cm wide.

Making up the dress

1 You will need: Enough narrow lace to finish the hem and bodice edges of the dress, and the frills – probably 5 metres altogether.
Spool of elastic thread.
Seam allowance: 1.5cm

2 Press a 0.5cm turning to the *right* side along the hemline and upper edge of the dress. Lay the narrow lace over the turning and machine hem and lace together in a zig-zag stitched seam *(figure 117)*.

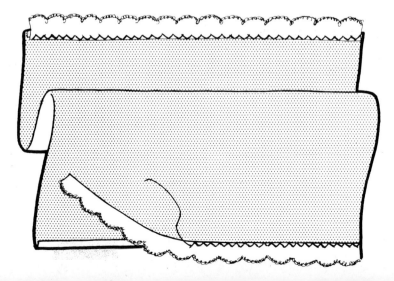

Figure 117

12 Shirred dress from nightie *(left)* and sundress

3 Finish one edge of each frill in the same way.

4 Gather the frills as shown in *figure 91* (for the Long Pinafore). Along each edge of the shoulder straps, fold in 1cm; then fold in half again and press. Slot the gathered edge of the frill between the folded edges of the strap, and top-stitch *(figure 118)*.

5 The bodice shirring is worked with elastic thread wound by hand on to the machine bobbin. Set the longest machine stitch you can. Stitch with the right side of the fabric uppermost, so that the elastic thread is on the wrong side. Machine first 2cm from the upper edge of the bodice, then at 2cm intervals. Work 7 (8, 9) rows of shirring altogether *(figure 119)*. If the elastic does not draw up the fabric tightly enough, pull the threads up on the wrong side until the bodice fits.

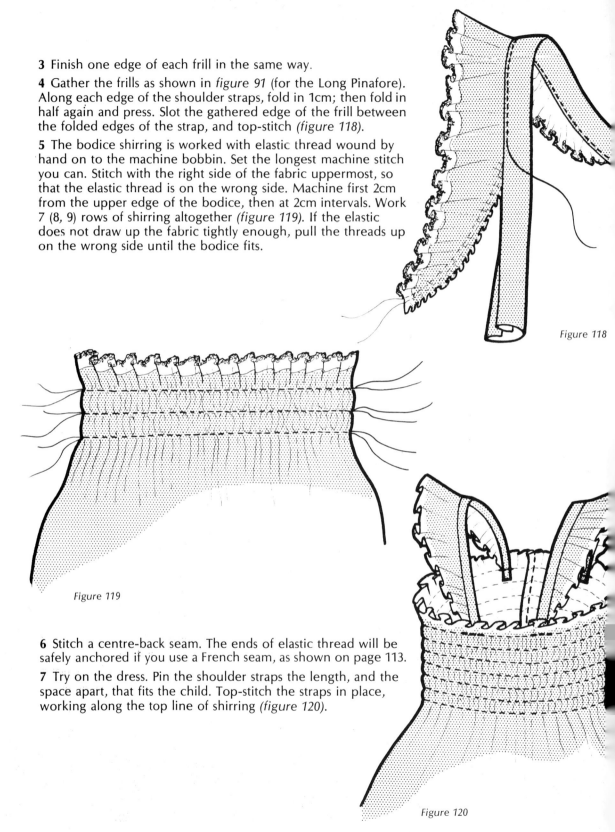

Figure 118

Figure 119

6 Stitch a centre-back seam. The ends of elastic thread will be safely anchored if you use a French seam, as shown on page 113.

7 Try on the dress. Pin the shoulder straps the length, and the space apart, that fits the child. Top-stitch the straps in place, working along the top line of shirring *(figure 120)*.

Figure 120

Sundress

Sizes 5 (6, 7)

Halter ties, and an elasticated back waistline, give a snug fit to this little charmer. It uses the minimum of fabric and could be cut from a blouse, a summer skirt or from dressmaking scraps. The one shown at the right on page 91 was made from a spare piece of curtaining cotton.

Drafting the pattern

The front

Cut a rectangle of paper 48 (52, 56) cm long by 24 (24.5, 25) cm wide
Mark the corners A, B and C as in *figure 121*
Measuring down the right-hand edge:
A – D is 6
A – E is 10
Measuring along the top edge:
A – F is 4.5
A – G is 8.5

H is 1.5 below F
J is 9.5 to the left of E
B – K down the left-hand edge is 20
L is 6 to the right of K
At the bottom left-hand corner:
M is 2 above C
N is 15 to the right of C
Join F – H – D for the neckline. (F – H is a straight line; H – D is a quarter circle)
Join G – J – L for the bodice sides. (G – J is a straight line; J – L is almost a quarter circle)
Join L – M for the side seam
Join M – N for the hemline
Cut out, discarding the shaded areas
Mark a fold-arrow down the right-hand edge

The back

Cut a rectangle of paper 29 (33, 37) cm long by 25.5 (26, 26.4) cm wide

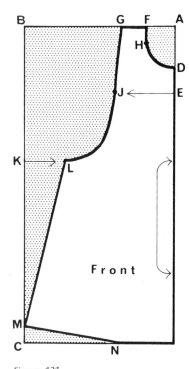

Figure 121

Mark the corners A, B and C as shown in *figure 122.*
A – D down the left-hand edge is 6.5
Measuring along the top edge:
B – E is 12.5
B – F is 16
G is 4 below F
At the bottom right-hand corner:
H is 4 above C
J is 15 to the left of C
Join D – G – E for the waistline
Join E – H for the side seam
Join H – J for the hemline
Cut out, discarding the shaded areas
Mark a fold-arrow down the left-hand edge

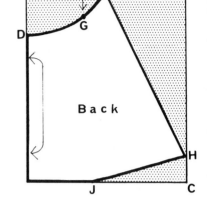

Figure 122

Cutting out

If you are short of fabric, a seam can be added at the centre-back (see page 110). Cut two halter straps 30cm long by 10cm wide.

Making up the sundress

1 You will need: 1.5 metres of broderie anglaise trimming 10cm wide for the hemline; and 20cm for the pocket.
1.2 metres of broderie anglaise 3cm wide for the bodice.
1 metre of white bias binding.
20cm narrow elastic.
12cm narrow white tape.

2 Stitch the side seams.

3 Seam together the ends of the wide broderie anglaise. Gather it to fit and stitch it round the hemline. (See page 113 for gathering instructions.)

4 Stitch the elastic inside the back waistline, from side seam to side seam, stretching it to fit *(figure 123).* Check the fit on the child.

5 Gather the narrow broderie anglaise to fit the bodice sides and back waistline, and tack it in place on the right side. Finish with bias binding (page 112) to enclose the raw edges and the elastic.

6 Finish the front neckline with bias binding.

Figure 123

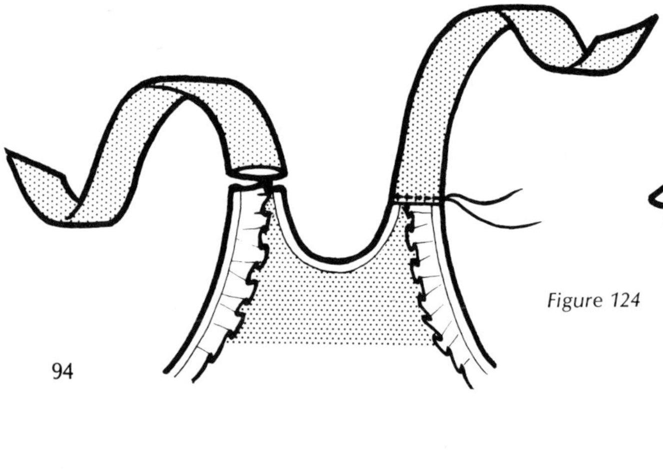

Figure 124

94

7 Fold the halter straps right sides together. Taking only 1cm seam turnings, stitch the long side and make a pointed end. Trim, turn right side out and press. Turn in 1cm at the unfinished end. The straps should have a finished width of 4cm, to fit over the shoulder edges of the bodice. Slot these edges into the strap ends and top-stitch *(figure 124)*.

8 Make up the pocket. Gather the unfinished edge of the broderie anglaise tightly, to form the bottom of the pocket. Gather 2cm below the top edge, draw it up to 12cm and stitch the gathers over the tape *(figure 125)*. Turn in the side edges 1cm and press.

9 Try on the dress to decide the position of the pocket. Stitch the lower gathered edge to the dress, as shown in *figure 126*. Fold the pocket upwards and top-stitch its sides.

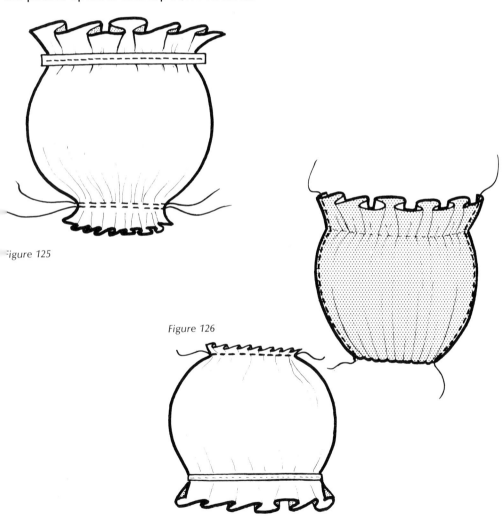

Figure 125

Figure 126

Beach Anorak from Stretchable Towelling Dressing Gown

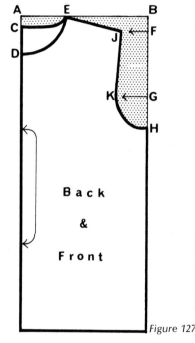

Figure 127

Sizes 5/7 (8/10, 11/12)

The anorak shown opposite – indispensable for English beaches – is designed for stretchable towelling and is one of those garments that will grow with the child from one summer to the next. Do not use ordinary terry towelling, as its lack of stretch would call for wider fitting and a neck opening.

Drafting the pattern

The back and front

Cut a rectangle of paper 48 (53, 58) cm long by 20 (24, 28) cm wide
Mark its top corners A and B as shown in *figure 127*.
Measuring down the left-hand edge:
A – C is 1.5
A – D is 6
Measuring along the top edge, A – E is 7
Measuring down the right-hand edge:
B – F is 2
B – G is 12
B – H is 17

J is 4 to the left of F
K is 5 to the left of G
Join C – E for the back neckline
Join D – E for the front neckline; this is almost a quarter circle
Join E – J for the shoulder seam
Join J – K – H for the armhole. (J – K is a straight line; K – H is a quarter circle)
Cut out, discarding the shaded areas for the back pattern
Mark a fold-arrow down the left-hand side
On fresh paper, trace round this pattern, mark the lower neckline and cut out the front pattern.

The sleeves

Cut a rectangle 20cm wide by 38 (40, 44) cm long
Mark A and B at the top and bottom left-hand corners, as in *figure 128*.
C is 10.5 to the right of A
D is 5 below A
E is 9 to the right of B

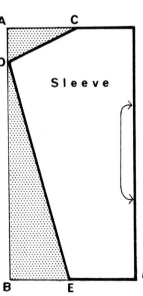

Figure 1

13 Beach anorak from stretchable towelling dressing gown

Join C – D for the sleevehead
Join D – E for the side seam
Cut out, discarding the shaded areas
Mark a fold-arrow down the right-hand edge

The hood

Cut a rectangle of paper 22cm wide by 27 (29, 30) cm long
Mark the corners A, B and C as shown in *figure 129*.
A – D along the top edge is 10
A – E down the left-hand edge is 10
B – F along the bottom edge is 4
G is 1.5 above F
Join D – E – G for the hood seam. (D – E is a quarter circle;
E – G is a straight line)
Join C – G for the neckline
Cut out, discarding the shaded areas
Mark a straight-grain arrow parallel to the right-hand edge

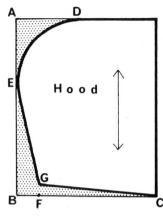

Figure 129

Cutting out

If you are cutting from an adult's dressing gown, you should get
the whole front of the anorak from the back of the gown. In the
two larger sizes, you may need to add a centre-back seam
(see page 110) and cut a half-back from each front of the gown
(figure 130).

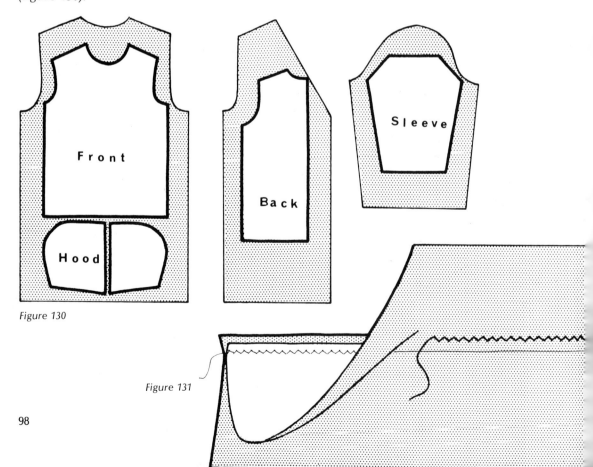

Figure 130

Figure 131

Making up the anorak

1 You will need 20cm narrow tape.
Seam allowance: 1.5cm   Hem allowance: 3cm.

2 Use double-stitched zig-zag for all seams (straight stitching for shoulder seams only). Stitch first with right sides together. Press turnings to one side, trim the underneath turning to half its width and top-stitch 1cm from the first stitching *(figure 131)*.

3 Stitch the back seam of the hood. Stitch a seam 4cm long at the centre-front neckline and press its edges open. Turn in a hem round the hood opening and stitch from the wrong side *(figure 132)*.

4 Stitch the shoulder seams, reinforcing them with tape as these are the only seams which must not stretch *(figure 133)*.

5 Stitch the hood into the neckline, matching the centre-fronts *(figure 134)*.

6 Stitch the sleeveheads to the armholes *(figure 135)*.

7 Stitch the side and sleeve seams as one *(figure 136)*.

8 Turn up and stitch the hems at wrist and hipline.

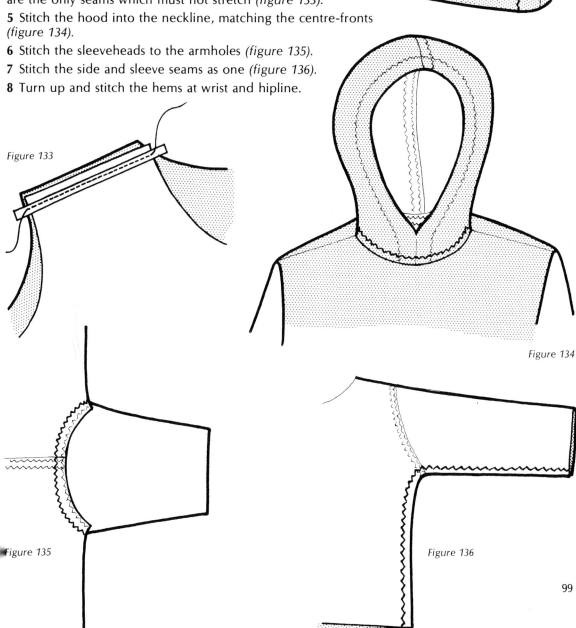

Figure 132

Figure 133

Figure 134

Figure 135

Figure 136

Baby-Doll Pyjamas
from Dirndl Skirt

Sizes 8/9 (10/11)

The baby-doll pyjamas shown on the right opposite were formerly a gathered cotton skirt, mid-calf-length with a border print. This, unpicked into a single length of fabric, gave plenty of room for the pyjamas in either size. The problem with a border print is to place it to the best advantage, which may mean adding seams to some pattern pieces.

The fit of these pyjamas is given by elastic, so they will grow with their wearer for at least two years.

Drafting the pattern

The front

Cut a rectangle of paper 24 (25.5) cm wide by 45 (48) cm long
Mark the top corners A and B as shown in *figure 137*.
A – C down the left-hand edge is 18
A – D along the top edge is 8
B – E down the right-hand edge is 3
Join C – D for the raglan armhole
Join D – E in a shallow curve for the neckline
Cut out, discarding the shaded areas
Mark a fold-arrow down the right-hand edge

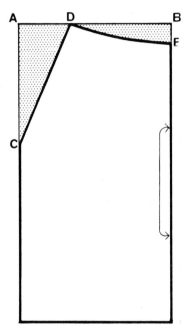

Figure 137

The back

The same as the front, but omitting the neckline shaping D – E

The sleeves

Cut a rectangle of paper 25 (30) cm long by 15cm wide
Mark the top left-hand corner A, as in *figure 138*.
A – B down the left-hand edge is 18
A – C along the top edge is 8
Join B – C for the raglan armhole
Cut out, discarding the shaded area
Mark a fold-arrow down the right-hand edge

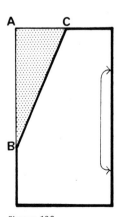

Figure 138

14 Baby-doll pyjamas from dirndl skirt *(right)* and popover pyjamas from two T-shirts

The pants

Cut a rectangle of paper 64 (67) cm wide by 32.5 (35) cm long
Mark the corners A, B, C, D as shown in *figure 139*.
A – E along the top edge is 8.5
B – F along the top edge is 5.5
G is 1.5 below F

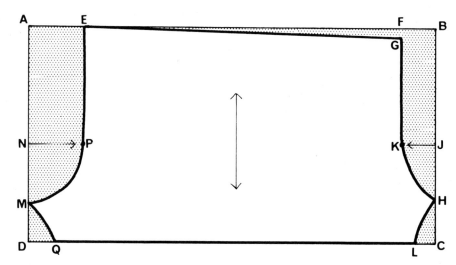

Figure 139

Measuring up the right-hand edge:
C – H is 7
C – J is 15

K is 5.5 to the left of J
L is 3 to the left of C
Measuring up the left-hand edge:
D – M is 6
D – N is 15

P is 8.5 to the right of N
Q is 4 to the right of D
Join E – G for the waistline edge
Join G – K – H for the front seam. (G – K is a straight line; K – H is a
shallow curve)
Join H – L in a slight curve for the front of the leg seam
Join E – P – M for the back seam. (E – P is a straight line; P – M is
almost a quarter circle)
Join M – Q in a slight curve for the back of the leg seam
Cut out, discarding the shaded areas
Mark a straight-grain arrow down the centre of the pattern

Cutting out

It is assumed – just to make it more difficult – that you are
working with a border print. The layout suggested in *figure 140*
places the lower edges of the front and of the pants along the
border.

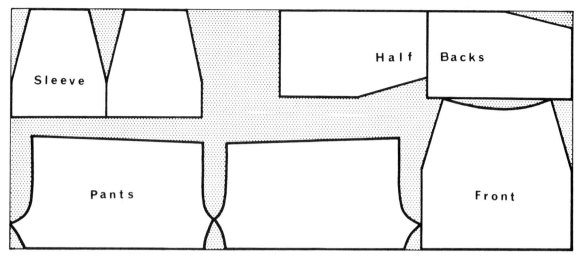

Figure 140

If you cannot fit such large pattern pieces on the available fabric, any of them (except the front) could have a seam added down the centre, as shown on page 110. Here, the top is seamed down the centre-back.

If you should be making these pyjamas from bought fabric, you would need 1.8 (1.9) metres of fabric 92cm wide.

Making up the pyjamas

1 You will need 2 metres of narrow elastic.
Seam allowance: 1.5cm.
2 Use French seams throughout (page 113). Stitch the four armhole seams. Stitch the sleeve and side edges as one continuous seam. Make the seam as narrow as possible at the armhole.

3 Stitch 0.5cm hems along the neck and sleeve edges. (Press a 1cm turning to the wrong side, tuck in the raw edge and machine.) See *figure 141*.

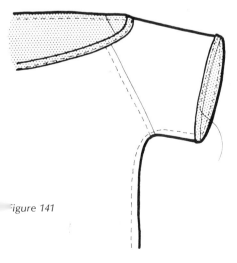

Figure 141

4 Cut a 45cm length of elastic, seam its ends together and zig-zag stitch it inside the neckline just below the hem, stretching it well as you machine.

5 Cut elastic strips to fit the child's arms and machine them 2cm above the sleeve edges, to make a frill *(figure 142)*.

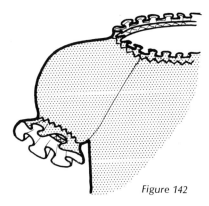

Figure 142

6 Turn up and machine a 2cm hem round the lower edge.

7 Stitch the centre-back and centre-front seams of the pants. Stitch the short seam across the crutch *(figure 143)*.

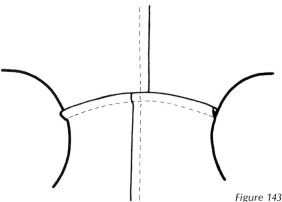

Figure 143

8 Along the waistline, press under a 2.5cm turning for the elastic casing. (As in *figure 52*, for jeans.) Thread in the elastic and fit it to the child's waist.

9 Finish the leg edges like the sleeves, with elastic 2.5cm above narrow hems.

Popover Pyjamas
from Two T-Shirts

Sizes 2 (3, 4)

Cotton jersey pyjamas that pull on over the head are more comfortable than buttoned ones and stay in place better on a small wriggling child. They are very simple to make and, with a little ingenuity, can be cut from two T-shirts. The ones shown on the left of page 101, in navy and white, are decorated with a predatory pussy-cat and a smug, safely-distanced mouse.

Drafting the pattern

The back

Cut a rectangle of paper 35 (36.5, 38.5) cm long by 16.5 (17, 17.5) cm wide
Mark the top corners A and B as in *figure 144*.
A – C down the left-hand edge is 2
B – D along the top edge is 11
B – E down the right-hand edge is 15
Join C – D in a shallow curve for the neckline
Join D – E for the raglan armhole
Cut out, discarding the shaded areas
Mark a fold-arrow down the left-hand edge

The front

Cut a rectangle of paper 32.5 (34, 36) cm long by 17.5 (18, 18.5) cm wide
Mark the top corners A and B as in *figure 145*.
A – C down the left-hand edge is 12.5
A – D along the top edge is 12.5
B – E down the right-hand edge is 5
Join C – D for the raglan armhole
Join D – E in a full curve for the neckline
Cut out, discarding the shaded areas
Mark a fold-arrow down the right-hand edge

The sleeves

Cut a rectangle of paper 38.5 (41, 44) cm long by 25.5cm wide
Mark the top corners A and B as in *figure 146*.

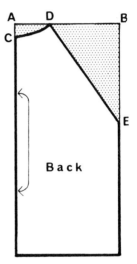

Figure 144

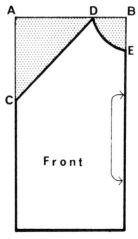

Figure 145

105

A – C down the left-hand edge is 17
A – D along the top edge is 8.5
B – E along the top edge is 6.5
F is 2 below E
B – G down the right-hand edge is 17
Join C – D for the back edge of the raglan shoulder
Join D – F in a shallow curve for the neckline
Join F – G for the front edge of the raglan shoulder
Cut out, discarding the shaded areas
Mark a straight-grain arrow between C and G

The pants

Cut a rectangle of paper 56 (60, 64) cm long by 42.5 (43.5, 44.5) cm wide
Mark the corners A, B, C, D as in *figure 147*.
Measuring down the left-hand edge:
A – E is 12 (13, 14)
E – F is 8.5

G is 7.5 to the right of E
A – H along the top edge is 7.5
B – J along the top edge is 5
Measuring down the right-hand edge:
B – K is 12 (13, 14)
K – L is 8

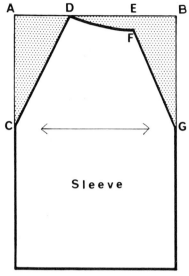

Figure 146

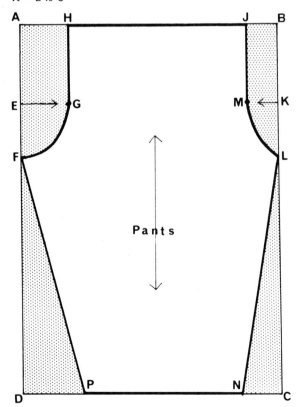

Figure 147

106

M is 5 to the left of K
Measuring along the bottom edge:
N is 6 to the left of C
P is 9.5 to the right of D
Join H – G – F for the back seamline. (H – G is a straight line)
Join F – P for the back edge of the inside leg seam
Join J – M – L for the front seamline. (J – M is a straight line)
Join L – N for the front edge of the inside leg seam
Cut out, discarding the shaded areas
Mark a straight-grain arrow down the centre of the pattern

Cutting out

From the dark T-shirt cut the pyjama pants as shown in
figure 148. If the shirt is not long enough, add at the ankle a
contrasting band from the light-coloured shirt.
Cut a neckline binding 42cm long by 6cm wide, and two sleeve
bindings 25cm long by 6cm wide, from the sleeves of the shirt.
Reserve a scrap of fabric for the mouse appliqué.

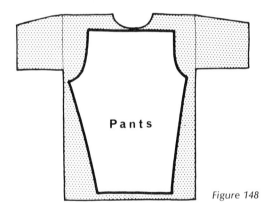

Figure 148

From the light T-shirt cut the pyjama top. You will probably need
to use the layout shown in *figure 149*. Cut ankle-bands, if
necessary, from the sleeves of the shirt. Reserve a scrap of fabric
for the cat appliqué.

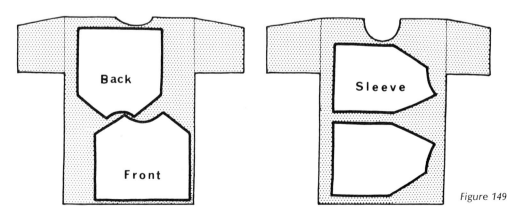

Figure 149

Making the pyjamas

1 You will need:
50cm elastic 1cm wide.
Embroidery cotton to match both T-shirts.
Seam allowance: 1cm only.

2 All seams should be zig-zag stitched. Press the turnings to one side and finish with top-stitching 0.5cm from the seamline, through all thicknesses.

3 Stitch the four raglan shoulder seams of the top *(figure 150)*.

4 With right sides together, stitch the cuff-bindings to the sleeves. Stitch the side and sleeve seam as one continuous seam. Turn the raw edge of the cuff binding to the inside and top-stitch just below the first seam, through all thicknesses, with zig-zag stitching *(figure 151)*. Trim close to the stitching.

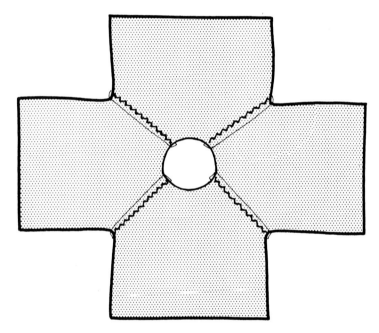

Figure 151

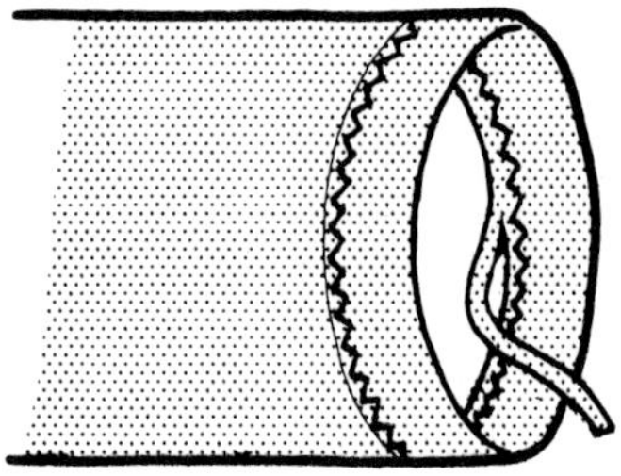

Figure 150

5 Stitch together the ends of the neckline binding, and press the turnings open. You may need to shorten the binding to fit the child's neck; make it big enough to stretch comfortably over the head.

6 With right sides together, zig-zag stitch the binding to the neckline. It will need to be stretched considerably. Turn in and finish as for the sleeves.

7 Turn up a 2cm hem, stitch and trim to the stitching.

8 If you are lengthening the pyjama legs with contrasting binding, stitch on the strips first.

9 Stitch the front and back seams of the pants, from waistline to crutch. Stitch the leg seams as one continuous seam, from ankle to crutch to ankle.

10 Turn in a 2cm casing along the waistline. Stitch twice, as shown in *figure 152*, leaving a short opening. Slot in the elastic and adjust to fit the child's waist.

11 Turn up the trouser bottoms in a 3cm hem – or to the length needed – and zig-zag stitch.

12 Trace the cat and mouse outlines from *figure 153* on to scraps of the contrasting fabrics. Cut them out with 1cm margins and sew in place (matching the grain of the fabrics) with small running stitches along the traced outline. Work close blanket-stitching over the running stitches, cutting off the margin only a short distance ahead of your needle to prevent a ragged edge. Put in details of eyes, whiskers etc. in the contrasting thread.

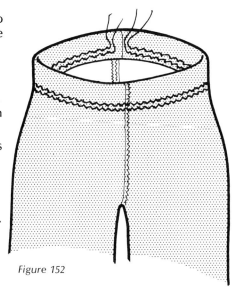

Figure 152

Figure 153

109

General Instructions

These instructions are for dressmaking processes common to several of the patterns in the book. They are collected here to save repetition.

Adding seams to patterns

After you have cut a paper pattern, extra seams may be added for styling or simply to make the pattern fit the fabric available.

1 Draw the line of the new seam on the pattern.

2 Cut the pattern along this line to separate the pieces *(figure 154)*.

3 Pin each piece over a strip of paper projecting from the new seamline. Mark a seam allowance of 1.5cm along that edge *(figure 155)*. Cut out.

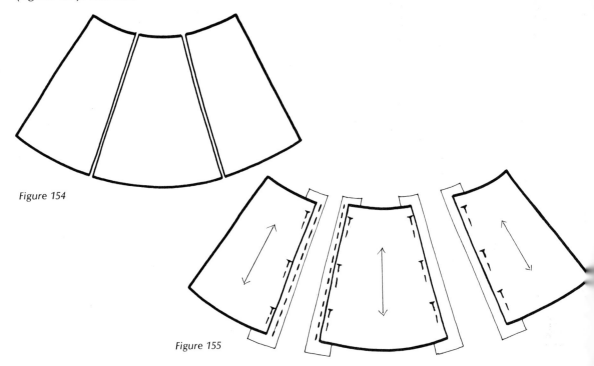

Figure 154

Figure 155

4 The straight grain should normally run down the centre of the pattern piece; add straight-grain arrows as necessary.

Using a garment's existing seams

Often, a pattern piece cannot be placed on a garment without crossing a seam. Where you have a straight seam, there is no reason you should not incorporate it, suitably placed, into a child's garment. You could, for instance, place it down the centre-back of a bodice.

If there are two pattern pieces which it would be convenient to place together, overlap and pin their seam allowances and put the joined pattern on the fabric, matching the join along the existing seam. Cut out as one piece *(figure 156)*.

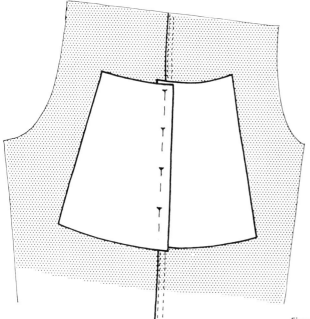

Figure 156

Adding width to a pattern

If a pattern size is right for your child's height, but is not wide enough round the chest, waist or hips, add extra width in this way.

1 Measure the extra width needed.

2 Down the side edges of the back and front patterns, add a *quarter* of this extra width. It will be a matter of merely 0.5cm-1cm, as the difference between one size and the next larger one is only 2-4cm. So you may be able just to cut the fabric that amount wider down the side of the pattern pieces, without altering the pattern itself, *figure 157*. (If you widen the bodice at the armhole, you should also widen the upper sleeve to match.)

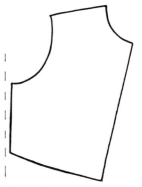

Figure 157

3 If you have to add more width than this, the pattern should be cut down the centre, separated and pinned the necessary distance apart over a strip of paper *(figure 158)*.

Bias binding

1 Cut strips for binding diagonally across the grain of the fabric, so that they are stretchable. The width normally needed, about 3cm, is conveniently the width of a ruler; so you can draw along both edges to mark out the strips *(figure 159)*.

2 Join the strips, if necessary, as shown in *figure 160*.

3 Press the edges to the centre along the length of the binding.

4 Unfold one edge. Match it to the edge of the garment, right sides together, and stitch along the crease *(figure 161)*.

5 Turn the binding over to the inside of the garment and hem the other crease just above the line of stitching *(figure 162)*.

6 For an all-round neckline or sleeve binding, finish by turning in the end and hemming it over the raw edge left at the beginning *(figure 163)*.

7 For binding that ends at an opening, such as at the top of a zip, fold in and finish as shown in *figure 164*.

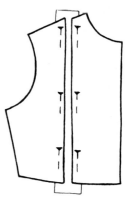

Figure 158

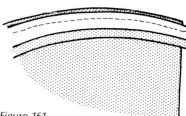

Figure 161

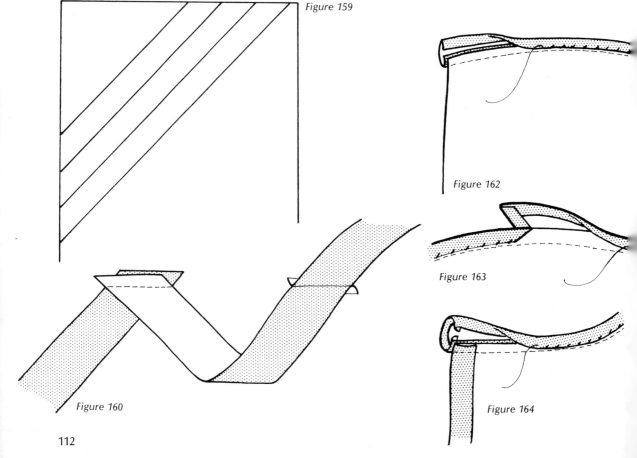

Figure 159

Figure 162

Figure 163

Figure 160

Figure 164

French seams

Suitable for a garment that is to be washed frequently, this seam is worked in two stages.

1 With wrong sides together, stitch 5mm from the edges *(figure 165)*.

2 Press the seam edges open.

3 With right sides together, fold along the stitching and press. Stitch again 1cm from the first stitching *(figure 166)*.

4 If you need to make a narrow French seam on a fine material, run the first line of stitching 1cm from the edges, trim the turnings to 3mm, then turn and stitch 5mm from the first stitching.

5 A very narrow seam, especially needed round a curve, can be stitched 1.2cm from the edges, trimmed to 2mm, and stitched again only 3mm from the first line of stitching.

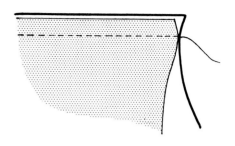

Figure 165

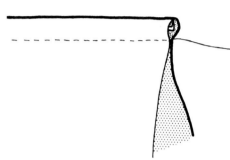

Figure 166

Gathering

1 In gathering up a wider piece of the garment to fit a narrower one, first run two lines of the longest machine stitching along the edge of the wider piece, one 1cm and the other 2cm from the edge.

2 Pull up the thread ends on the reverse of the fabric, until the gathered piece fits the narrower one *(figure 167)*.

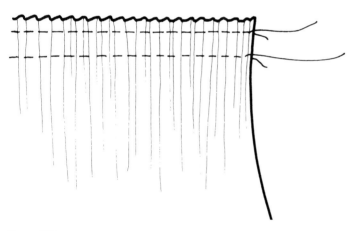

Figure 167

3 Pin together, adjusting the gathers evenly, and stitch 1.5cm from the edges *(figure 168)*.

4 Trim the raw edges and finish with zig-zag stitching.

5 Press the seam turning upwards, away from the gathers, and top-stitch from the right side if liked *(figure 169)*.

6 Pull out the gathering thread that shows on the right side.

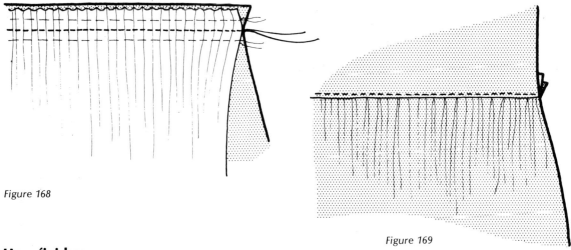

Figure 168

Figure 169

Hem finishes

On thin fabrics

1 Turn up the full depth of the hem to the wrong side. Fold in 1cm along the raw edge and press.

2 Tack in place.

3 Slip-hem as shown in *figure 170*, at each stitch taking only a thread or two of the garment, but making a longer stitch through the folded edge.

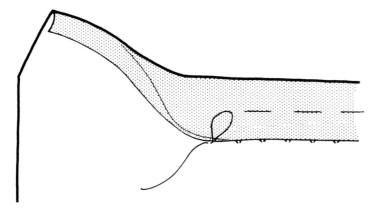

Figure 170

With lace

1 Press a 5mm turning to the *right* side of the garment edge.

2 With right sides up, lay the lace over the turning, and tack.

3 Stitch over the edge of the lace with machine satin stitch, a very short stitch set at medium width *(figure 171)*.

4 If the lace is to be gathered to the hem, follow the instructions for gathering, above.

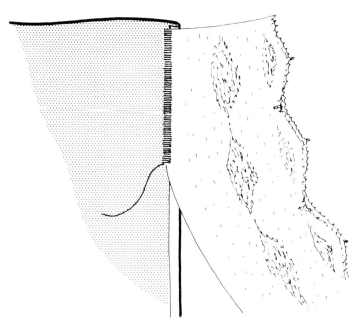

Figure 171

On thick fabrics

1 Finish the raw edge with zig-zag stitching.

2 Turn up the hem and tack.

3 Work catch-stitch between the two layers, as shown in figure 172.

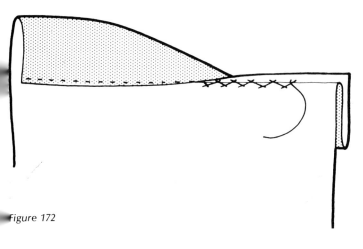

Figure 172

4 If your machine has a blind-hemming stitch, work this instead. Stitch along the single thickness of the turning, allowing only the swing-stitch to catch into the fabric of the garment (figure 173).

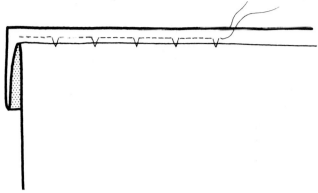

Figure 173

On thick fabric with binding

1 Stitch bias binding along the raw edge of the hem. Press upwards *(figure 174)*.

2 Turn up and tack the hem.

3 Slip-hem the free fold of the binding to the garment. This avoids the bulk of a doubled turning on thick fabric.

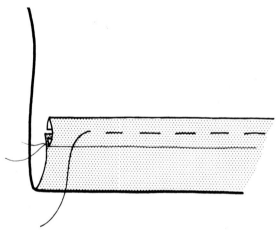

Figure 174

Machine-made buttonholes

These buttonholes can be worked quickly and easily on any woven fabric – always through two thicknesses.

1 Mark the buttonhole placings, evenly spaced, with tailor's chalk or pencil.

2 Set the machine needle to the left-hand position.

3 Slightly loosen the needle-thread tension.

4 Set the stitch at just under half its maximum width, and at a very short length. Test on a scrap of fabric; you should produce a close satin stitch, but not so close that the thread builds up into a knob on the back of the fabric.

5 Stitch along the left-hand side of the marking, ending with the needle down in the fabric, at the right-hand end of its swing *(figure 175)*.

6 Raise the presser-foot and pivot the buttonhole on the needle *(figure 176)*.

7 Lower the presser-foot. Raise the needle out of the work.

8 Set the widest stitch possible, and work five or six stitches at the same spot, across the end of the buttonhole *(figure 177)*.

9 Raise the needle, set the narrower width of stitch and work the second side. Be careful not to catch in the stitching of the first side *(figure 178)*.

10 Work the wider stitches at the second end of the buttonhole, as before *(figure 179)*.

11 Pull the thread ends through to the wrong side, knot them, thread them into a needle and lead them away between the two thicknesses of fabric.

12 With a seam-ripper, slit the buttonhole open, cutting from ends to middle to prevent accidents *(figure 180)*.

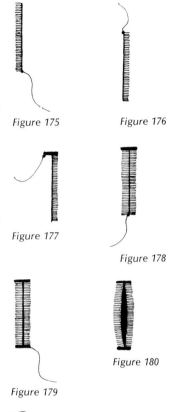

Figure 175

Figure 176

Figure 177

Figure 178

Figure 179

Figure 180

Setting in sleeves

1 Gather the upper half of the sleevehead *(figure 181)*.

2 Match each sleeve to its armhole. (The front edge of the sleevehead is hollowed out near the underarm; the back edge is cut wider.) See *figure 182*.

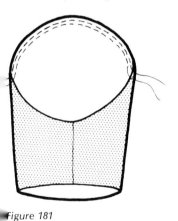

Figure 181

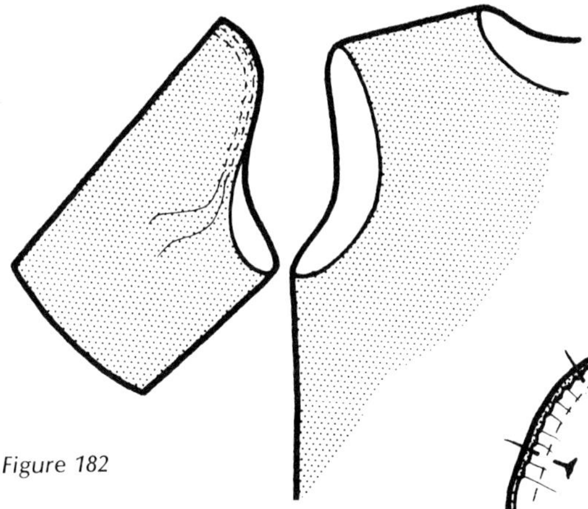

Figure 182

3 Turn the bodice inside out over the sleeve.

4 Pin as shown in *figure 183*, pulling up the gathers to fit the armhole. Match the underarm seams, and match the centre of the sleevehead to the shoulder seam.

5 Stitch 1.5cm from the edges. (In jersey fabrics, use a zig-zag stitch.)

6 Trim the raw edges and finish with zig-zag stitching or bias binding.

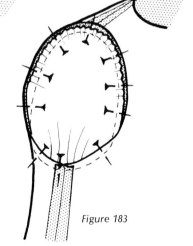

Figure 183

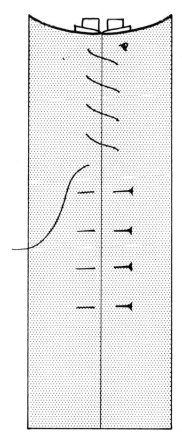

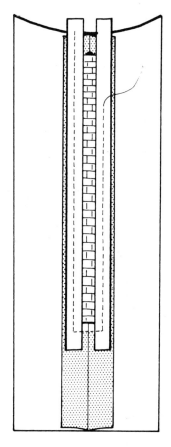

Figure 184   Figure 185

Setting in a zip

1 Machine-baste together the sides of the zip opening, using the longest stitch your machine will make. Press the turnings apart.

2 With right sides up, place the zip under the basted opening. Pin from the right side, through all thicknesses, as shown in *figure 184*. The zip should be centred behind the basting, with the top of the slider 1.5cm below the neckline edge. Baste the zip in place by hand and remove the pins.

3 On the wrong side, with a zipper-foot on the machine, stitch down one side of the zipper tape, across the bottom and up the other side *(figure 185)*.

4 Remove both sets of basting threads.

Index